BEHIND FACADES

BEHIND FACADES

ART BY

PAUL DRAPER

TEXT BY

TREWIN COPPLESTONE

MACMILLAN • USA

MACMILLAN
A Simon & Schuster Macmillan Company
15 Columbus Circle
New York, NY 10023

A MARSHALL EDITION
Designed and edited by
Marshall Editions
170 Piccadilly, London W1V 9DD

EDITOR
Gwen Rigby
ART DIRECTOR
John Bigg
ART EDITOR
Helen Spencer
PICTURE DIRECTOR
Zilda Tandy
PICTURE EDITOR
Richard Philpott
CONCEPT
Katherine Harkness

Macmillan is a registered trademark of Macmillan, Inc.

Library of Congress Cataloging-in-Publication Data

Draper, Paul.
Behind facades / Paul Draper, Trewin Copplestone.
p. cm.
ISBN 0-02-860431-8
1. Decoration and ornament, Architectural. 2. Interior architecture.
3. Decoration and ornament. 4. Interior decoration.
I. Copplestone, Trewin. II. Title.
NA3320.D73 1995
729—dc20 95-2736
CIP

Origination by Sele, Italy
Printed and bound in Italy by
Officine Grafiche De Agostini – Novara

2 4 6 8 10 9 7 5 3 1

CONTENTS

$\mathscr{I}$NTRODUCTION

A FACADE IS LIKE A MYSTERY: AN enigmatic exterior presenting tantalizing clues – or false clues – as to what lies behind its walls, windows, and doors. But whether or not the interior has the size, proportions, and decor suggested by its facade can only be discovered by going inside. The interior may confirm the exterior appearance or present a different, more surprising character that can be explained only by learning about the history of the building and about its architects and owners.

This book is concerned as much with what lies behind the facade as with the facade itself. And often the differences between the two provide a truly fascinating contrast.

The architectural consistency of the exterior or the adherence to a particular style – the Classical style, for instance, which is most frequently found in Western architecture – is not necessarily reflected in the interior. Great buildings achieve their own unique character through the changing tastes of succeeding generations of owners. And it is this sense of stylistic idiosyncrasy that inspires the curiosity most of us feel when looking at or walking through the rooms of a large or important building.

The intriguing unpredictability of the relationship between facade and interior is the genesis of this book, which includes examples of both consistency and dramatic variety in the buildings considered. For instance, the Virginia home of Thomas Jefferson, Monticello, displays a remarkable consistency of style; whereas the Cathedral Church of St. Peter in Rome, which took 150 years to complete, shows clear evidence of changing architectural tastes.

Five important buildings are discussed here: St. Peter's; Monticello; Buckingham Palace, London; the Opéra Garnier, Paris; and the castle of Neuschwanstein in Germany. Each is revealed in terms of the facade it presents to the world as well as through the interiors it conceals.

But before examining them individually, it is necessary to understand something of the historical context and the architectural terms used to describe them. And since all have distinct stylistic characteristics, some general clarification will be useful.

Throughout history, and throughout the world, there have been considerable variations in architectural styles. In the broadest terms, Eastern styles, such as Chinese and Indian architectural forms, can easily be recognized and distinguished from the architecture typical of the Western world. In the case of the buildings considered here, the text will explore and

THE PARTHENON (447–432 B.C.) *on the Acropolis, dominating the city of Athens, is probably the best-known building in the Western world. It is in the Doric style and is the epitome of Classical refinement.*

illuminate the different styles that have developed within the Western architectural tradition over the centuries.

Although there are just two distinct styles with which this book is concerned – Classical and Medieval – these in turn can be divided into sub-styles. Offshoots of the Classical style, for example, include the Palladian and the Baroque.

The Classical style itself derives from the ancient civilizations of Greece and Rome. Greek society, particularly that of Athens in the fifth century B.C., is regarded by many modern Western scholars as the cornerstone of political democracy. It also produced a veritable galaxy of philosophers, dramatists, poets, historians, natural scientists, artist-craftsmen, and architects, whose work is still read, performed, studied, and admired today.

By contrast, the Romans were a down-to-earth, pragmatic people who carved out the largest empire in antiquity, impressing their conquered territories with their own cultural stamp. They were also great engineers and builders, as made evident by

THE PANTHEON (A.D. 120–24), *the most perfectly preserved ancient Roman building, is composed of a domed rotunda with a pedimented, columned portico.*

the amphitheaters, aqueducts, and other civic structures that can still be seen throughout Europe, Asia Minor, and northern Africa.

The combined cultural influence of Greece and Rome has become known as Classical, and over the centuries its effect upon architecture has been far-reaching and tenacious. The four "Classical" buildings presented in this book were erected at different times over a period of more than 250 years, and buildings with distinctly Classical characteristics are still being designed today.

The Greeks established the Classical style by elaborating upon a method of building known as trabeation, which employs simple posts and a lintel. From the development of trabeation, most of the elements of Classical architecture were defined. Rules of proportion, forms of detailing, and patterns of decoration were, so to speak, cast in stone.

SALISBURY CATHEDRAL (1220–58) *is almost entirely in the 13th-century Early English style. The spire is the tallest in England (404 feet/123 m) and reflects the English preference for a spire at the point where the transept crosses the nave.*

The most recognizable elements of the Classical style are the "orders," or styles of architecture identified by the different types of column – along with its base, shaft, capital, and superstructure, or entablature – used by architects for temples and other buildings. Prominently used, one or other of these remains the recognizable feature of all Classical buildings, including St. Peter's, the Opéra Garnier, Monticello, and Buckingham Palace.

The Greeks used three such orders – the Doric, Ionic, and Corinthian – and the Romans adapted the Greek style to their own architectural needs, expanding its range. They developed their own versions of the Greek orders and added two of their own: the Tuscan and Composite. (*See pages 76–77 for more detail.*) However, their main architectural innovation was the use in

public buildings of the arch, and its circular extension, the dome, perhaps best seen in the Pantheon – the temple dedicated to all the Roman gods – in Rome.

During the first centuries A.D., the Christian Church began to emerge in different parts of the Roman Empire and, by the fourth century, it had become the official state religion. Despite its later fracture into a number of sects, it has remained the dominant faith of the Western world. And it has also given rise to the second major architectural style – the Medieval – which accompanied the growth of the religion and expanded into a great variety of structural and decorative forms.

Throughout its progressive alterations, Medieval architecture retained many common features that were different from those found on Classical buildings. These differences illuminate both the nature and origins of the styles.

For instance, whereas Classical architecture is founded on rational thought and intellectual confidence, Medieval structures

TRURO CATHEDRAL (1880–1910), *designed by the architect J.L. Pearson and not completed until 13 years after his death, represents the reconstruction of the Medieval church form, although unlike Salisbury it emphasizes the spires on the western towers.*

THE DOMED CHURCH *of Les Invalides in Paris (1693–1706), designed by J.H. Mansart in the form of a Greek cross with arms of equal length, reflects the growing use of Classical features in religious architecture.*

seem to embody religious aspiration, faith, and a yearning for the spiritual virtues represented by the life of Jesus Christ.

As a result, Medieval architecture emphasizes vertical forms, with spires, pointed arches, finials, and ribbed vaults. (The persistence of the style can be judged from the fact that Salisbury Cathedral, which dates from the thirteenth century, and Truro Cathedral – the last spired cathedral in Britain, built more than 600 years later – are both Medieval in appearance.)

As well as being linked with soaring cathedrals, the Middle Ages also have romantic secular associations: moated castles with turreted towers, and tales of knights errant. This emotional legacy lingered on in western Europe into the nineteenth century, and the last of the buildings considered here, Neuschwanstein, Ludwig II's castle in Bavaria, is one such romantic evocation: an extravaganza commemorating the medieval Teutonic legends of Parsifal, Siegfried, and Tannhäuser.

The medieval period – which lasted from about 1000 to 1500 – was one of unparalleled building activity. One writer has estimated that, in the three centuries from 1050 to 1350, several million tons of stone were quarried in France alone and formed the raw material for 80 cathedrals, and thousands of churches, large and small.

This era of Christian building was succeeded by another, the Renaissance, which developed in Italy during the fifteenth century and spread to other parts of Europe. The Renaissance looked back to Classical antiquity for its architectural inspiration, as it did for other aspects of culture. This revived "Classical" style was now used not only in the design of palaces, public buildings, and large and medium-sized houses, but also in places of Christian worship. Certainly, the greatest of all churches, St. Peter's, is an entirely Classical building.

Bramante, Raphael, and Michelangelo, the preeminent artists and architects of the Renaissance period, all contributed to the the church's final design. Indeed, Michelangelo's dome was to become the prototype and inspiration for many other domed

SIR CHRISTOPHER WREN *designed St. Paul's Cathedral (1675–1711) in London in a typically restrained English Classical Baroque style.*

CHISWICK HOUSE (c.1730) *was on the outskirts of London when it was built by Lord Burlington, who adapted one of Palladio's own designs. It represents a fine example of the Palladian style.*

churches, including perhaps the most famous of all Protestant churches, St. Paul's Cathedral in London, as well as the great church of Les Invalides in Paris.

The most influential of the Renaissance architects was, however, the Italian Andrea Palladio (1508–80), for whom a sub-style of Classical European architecture has been named. This Palladian style, which was prevalent primarily in England at the beginning of the eighteenth century, was also the dominant influence in the design for Monticello. Palladio's contribution was to modernize the Classical style while retaining its spirit. In 1570, showing considerable commercial acumen, he published his *I Quattro Libri dell'Architettura*, translated into English as *The Four Books of Architecture*. These contained many of his designs and became the most important work on Classical architecture.

Palladio lived and worked mainly in Vicenza, in the Republic of Venice, and three of his buildings in that area are of

THE VILLA ALMERICO (1566–71) *is illustrated in Palladio's* Quattro Libri, *thus providing a model for many later architects, notably Lord Burlington and Colen Campbell. It is square in plan, with a surmounting dome and porticoes on all four sides.*

particular interest in the context of this book: the Villa Almerico, also known as the Villa Rotonda, near Vicenza; the Palazzo Chiericati situated in the town; and the Villa Barbaro at Maser in the Veneto region. The importance of Palladian style was its flexibility: it could be adapted for a variety of social and religious purposes in different locations. At the same time, it still retained its Classical detailing and spirit.

Buckingham Palace is an interesting example of the late influence of Palladio. The familiar public facade seen from the Mall (the avenue that sweeps up to the palace from Trafalgar Square) is a pretentious elaboration of the winged villa. It is similar to the early eighteenth-century Villa Pisani at Stra, near Venice. The rarely seen garden facade of Buckingham Palace, designed in the 1820s by John Nash, is also part of the Palladian legacy by a different, more dignified and restrained, route.

The first notable extension of the Classical language of architecture took place in the seventeenth century with the style, or more properly sub-style, known as Baroque. Gianlorenzo Bernini, sculptor, painter, and architect, was the dominant creative figure and one of the greatest exponents of Baroque art in Rome. His brilliant creations in St. Peter's are responsible for much of the character of the interior of the building.

The Baroque is full of exuberance and exaggeration; it is expansive, imaginative, dynamic, and emotional, concerned less with control than with self-expression, as shown, for instance, by Baldassare Longhena's church of Santa Maria della Salute in Venice. So it is not surprising that it treated Classically based forms with less respect than was accorded to them during the Renaissance.

Baroque architecture developed into the delicate intricacies of the Rococo, and this style can be seen in many eighteenth-century Bavarian churches. It is found, for example, in the flamboyant interior of the

THE VILLA PISANI (1736) *is an example of the winged villa reduced to a near-flat facade, with pediments at each end and a central blind portico. This type of design is also found in many English country houses.*

Wies church by the brothers Domenikus and Johan Baptist Zimmermann.

A late expression of the Baroque in France is evident in the Paris Opéra, now known as the Opéra Garnier. Its fussy, grandiloquent use of the Classical orders and the ornate decoration of the facade and interior make it a unique example of what is usually described as French Neobaroque.

BUCKINGHAM PALACE (1825–46), *begun by John Nash, was the work of a number of architects. The present facade by Sir Aston Webb was completed in 1913 in Portland stone.*

The strong Classical influence evident in the first four buildings in this book emphasizes the dominance of Classicism in European architecture. As a fascinating, if bizarre, coda, an example of the Medieval influence is also included. During the nineteenth century, Medievalism became fashionable as an alternative to the constraints of Classical discipline, offering romantic notions associated with chivalric legends of a distant age. However, no truly medieval castle was ever like King Ludwig II's Neuschwanstein, whose crowded and eclectic interior resembles the Rococo of the Wies church nearby.

It has been said that a great building is a symphony composed in stone. This book offers five magnificent symphonies: the facade of each structure – re-created in meticulous detail – opens up to reveal the glories of the interior, giving a fresh perspective on five masterpieces of Western architecture and an insight into the minds of those who built them.

THE ZIMMERMANN BROTHERS *together designed both the church of the Wies in Bavaria (1746–54) and its interior decoration.*

THE CATHEDRAL CHURCH OF ST. PETER, ROME

"Thou art Peter, and upon this rock I will build my church; and the gates of hell shall not prevail against it…I will give unto thee the keys of the kingdom of heaven."

CHRIST'S WORDS, QUOTED IN ST. MATTHEW'S Gospel, lead directly to the story of the building of St. Peter's in Rome, the greatest church in Christendom. The cruel persecution of the Christians in the first century A.D. under the Emperor Nero, during which thousands died in the Colosseum to entertain Roman citizens, is part of the early known history of Christian martyrdom. And among those reputed to have died in Rome at this time was St. Peter, not torn apart by wild animals, but crucified head downward in the Circus of Nero. Although there is no direct evidence of Peter ever having been in Rome, the story has become enshrined in tradition.

Persecution of the Christians continued until 313 A.D., when the Emperor Constantine became a Christian; 20 years later he established Christianity as the official religion of the Roman Empire. Among Constantine's many acts was the construction of the first church dedicated to St. Peter, near the supposed site of St. Peter's martyrdom and above a cemetery in which he was believed to have been buried.

It is also part of the tradition of the Church that St. Peter was the first Bishop of Rome, and that the authority of all later popes has descended directly from him through what is known as the Apostolic Succession. St. Peter's has thus become the mother church of the Roman Catholic faith and the pope the ultimate interpreter of that faith.

By the time Nicholas V was elected pope in 1447, the urgent necessity for a new church to replace Constantine's ancient basilica had long been apparent. Despite much patching

THE ILLUSTRATION of the exterior of St. Peter's (*see previous page*) shows what is, in effect, a close-up of a distant view. It reveals the important elements of the cathedral in a way impossible for visitors to see as they approach across the vast piazza, since, close up, the facade creates a great screen across the front, obscuring the dome.

Contrasting strongly with the austere, imposing dignity of the facade is this splendid interior view along the nave, with its color and rich decoration. St. Peter's Chair in the apse is shown framed by the 66-foot-high (20-m) twisted columns of the *baldacchino* as Bernini had intended. The feeling of awesome power and pageantry inspired by the cathedral is as overwhelming today as it was when it was completed in the seventeenth century.

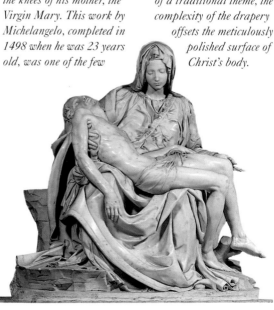

ON HIGH FESTIVAL DAYS, *the bronze figure of St. Peter, holding the keys to heaven and with its right hand raised in blessing, is decked in papal vestments, and the three-tiered papal crown is set upon its head. One of the most revered statues in the cathedral, it was once thought to be the earliest image of the saint, dating from the 5th century, but recent study suggests that it is the work of Arnolfo di Cambio and was cast between 1250 and 1275.*

THE MARBLE STATUE *known as the* Pietà *depicts the dead Christ lying on the knees of his mother, the Virgin Mary. This work by Michelangelo, completed in 1498 when he was 23 years old, was one of the few* sculptures he finished and *the only one he signed. In this sophisticated treatment of a traditional theme, the complexity of the drapery offsets the meticulously polished surface of Christ's body.*

GIANLORENZO BERNINI, shown in a self-portrait (below) dating from c.1655, was the greatest genius of the Italian Baroque, and his work, along with that of Michelangelo, was the most significant in creating the character and visual impact of St. Peter's.

The Cathedra Petri, or Chair of St. Peter (above), is a theatrical creation made by Bernini to house, within the bronze throne, a 6th-century wooden chair. At the base, gilt-bronze figures of the Fathers of the Church – Saints Ambrose, Athanasius, Chrysostom, and Augustine – support the throne. Above, gilt-bronze angels and sun rays, gilded stucco clouds, and a stained-glass window depicting the Dove (the symbol of the Holy Spirit) combine to produce one of the most dramatic and moving works in the church.

and restoration, the building was in a dilapidated and dangerous condition – more than one pope had had a narrow escape from falling stonework. None, however, had been courageous enough to replace a building that represented so much of the Church's early history and in which Charlemagne had been crowned Holy Roman Emperor on Christmas Day 800. Nicholas was the first to confront the problem.

Not only St. Peter's, but Rome itself, was in great need of rehabilitation, for the magnificent buildings of the Roman Empire were in serious decay after centuries of neglect. Nicholas embarked on a great program of rebuilding and restoration, with St. Peter's at the center of his concern. Although he recognized that a new church was needed, even he did not have the confidence to demolish the old basilica, and he compromised by planning a new building around it, with the idea of incorporating the old within the new. So the old church stood crumbling, but in use, throughout the subsequent building activity.

On Nicholas's instructions, the sculptor and architect Bernardo Rossellino began building – on an enormous scale – part of the intended sanctuary end of the new church outside the walls of the ancient basilica. (In many of Constantine's churches, including St. Peter's, the sanctuary was at the west end, not the east as is more usual.) Later popes discontinued the work, but the gigantic walls remained and determined the final scale of the new church. In this way, St. Peter's became not only the largest Christian church by far, but also the greatest building enterprise of the period in Europe, at times employing hundreds of laborers, stone workers, carvers, and other craftsmen.

Nicholas V was the first truly Renaissance pope, and his wish to restore the earlier glory and grandeur of imperial Rome was accompanied by a passion for all aspects of its culture, including its architecture. As a result, he favored the change from the old style of the great medieval cathedrals to the new Renaissance style derived from "classical" Greek and Roman architecture. St. Peter's was to become a Classical building.

Succeeding popes, although making plans for St. Peter's, did not carry the work forward, and Constantine's church continued

POPE JULIUS'S *portrait was painted by Raphael in 1512, at the same time that he was decorating apartments in the Vatican Palace. On Julius's orders, Raphael also prepared a plan for St. Peter's, which was approved but not used.*

THE ATMOSPHERE *of piety and pageantry always present in St. Peter's is captured in this view of a processional ceremony in the 1960s, which shows Pope Paul VI blessing the congregation as he is carried aloft down the nave.*

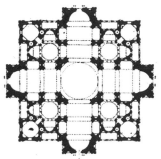

BRAMANTE'S *plan was based on a Greek cross, with four equal arms within a circle, providing a centralized plan, and with a large central dome. Work began in 1506.*

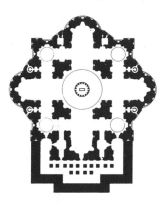

MICHELANGELO'S *design of 1547 modified Bramante's plan. The main church was squared off, the shape of the dome altered, and a portico and steps added at the east end.*

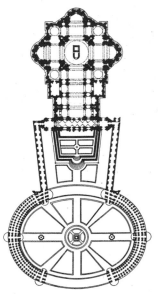

THE FINISHED CHURCH *shows the eastern arm extended into a long nave and an atrium and facade added by Maderno. The importance of Bernini's piazza and connecting colonnades is evident from the plan.*

PLAN OF ST. PETER'S TODAY

1 St. Peter's Chair (Bernini) **2** *Baldacchino* and papal altar (Bernini) **3** Tomb of Pope Alexander VII (Bernini) **4** Entrance to treasury **5** Portico (Maderno) **6** Medieval bronze door from old basilica of St. Peter's (Antonio Averlino) **7** Steps to main entrance platform **8** Holy door (open only in Holy years) **9** *Pietà* (Michelangelo) **10** Tabernacle on the altar of the Blessed Sacrament Chapel (Bernini) **11** Statue of St. Peter (medieval bronze) **12** Tomb of Pope Urban VIII (Bernini) **A** Four main piers for the dome (Bramante and Michelangelo) **B** Nave extension, portico, and facade (Maderno)

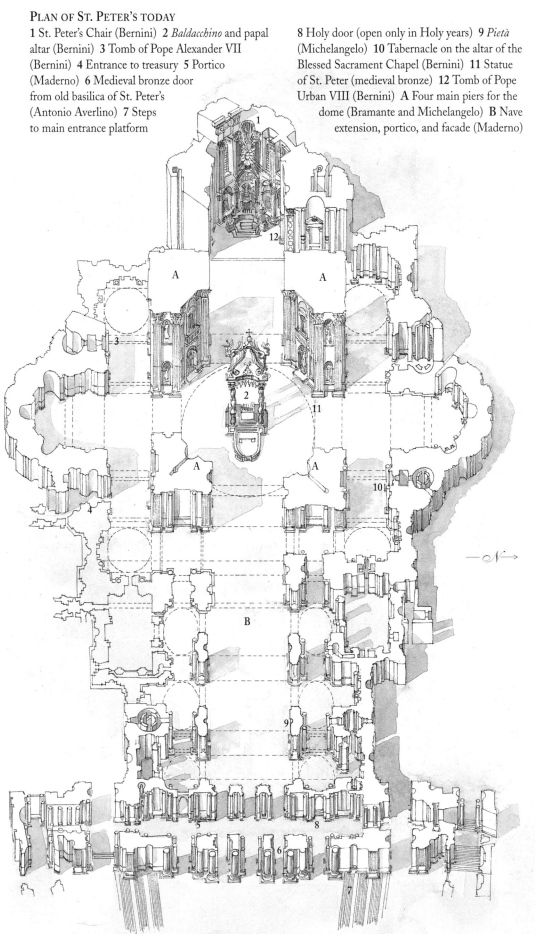

to be used, while behind it Rossellino's structure deteriorated. It was not until the early 1500s, under Pope Julius II, that purposeful rebuilding began again. Julius, known as the warrior pope because of his extensive military activity (notably against Bologna, which he annexed to the Papal States), was one of the strongest and most active popes. Under his rule, the Papal States became supreme in Italy and a great power in Europe.

At the same time Julius made Rome the center of European art, gathering around him most of the greatest artists and architects of the day, including Michelangelo, Leonardo da Vinci, Raphael, and Donato Bramante, the architect to whom he entrusted the task of redesigning St. Peter's. He also made the bold decision, avoided by his predecessors, to demolish Constantine's church and start with a new plan, incorporating Rossellino's earlier structure if possible. Bramante prepared a design that was accepted, and in April 1506 the pope laid the foundation stone of the new basilica. A medal showing the intended church was struck to commemorate the occasion.

When Julius died in 1513 and Bramante a year later, the old church had been partly demolished and the new building taken energetically forward. But little or no further work was done for 30 years until the pontificate of Paul III, who appointed Michelangelo Buonarroti – then age 72 – as Architect in Chief of St. Peter's in 1546. This project, on which for years work had been carried out only spasmodically, was to many a thankless and almost superhuman task, and one Michelangelo was reluctant to undertake.

Michelangelo had always described himself as a sculptor and wanted neither to paint nor to build. He was a morose, suspicious character, and Paul, fully aware of this from Julius's dealings with Michelangelo over the painting of the Sistine Chapel, gave him "full authority to change the model, form, and structure at will." This, and the fact that he insisted on working without payment, gave Michelangelo great authority in decision making, and freedom from his many professional enemies. His powerful will and immense energy meant that, by his death in 1564, at the age of 89, much of the central part of the church was finished and its eventual completion assured. Although the dome was

MICHELANGELO, *whose portrait was painted by Marcello Venusti, was responsible for a major part of the finished church of St. Peter, and it was his energy and dedication that brought the building to certain completion. He regarded his buildings as sculptures, molding and changing them as he went along, an approach that gave his architectural work originality, passion, and dynamism.*

THE VIEW *from the roof of the Vatican Museum shows the west end of St. Peter's. Jacopo Vignola built the two smaller domes in 1565; Giacomo Della Porta had, by 1590, completed the great dome, which dominates its surroundings as Michelangelo intended. He kept the drum, but raised the outer dome 25 feet (7.5 m), so it was more ovoid than in Michelangelo's final plan.*

BERNINI'S GREAT *elliptical colonnaded piazza and the gallery corridors that connect it with the cathedral facade give dramatic shape to this spectacular view across Rome. In the foreground, vast statues of Christ, John the Baptist, and the apostles define the roof line of the cathedral facade.*

THE PIERS TO SUPPORT *Bramante's dome were already half built when Michelangelo produced his plan for St. Peter's, and he incorporated them into his own design. This included a double-shelled dome raised on a drum in which double columns alternated with windows to allow light into the church. The decoration of the hemispherical interior dome, 138 feet (42 m) in diameter, was completed in the 1590s under Pope Clement VIII.*

To fill the spaces between the strongly defined gilded stucco ribs, Christ, the Virgin, saints, apostles, and angels were depicted in mosaics. These were arranged in six rows, diminishing in size toward the lantern. On the soffit, or underside, of the lantern, the figure of God appears among the clouds.

ST. PETER'S CHURCH • 23

incomplete when he died, it was finished by others 26 year later, in 1590.

The final stage in building the body of the church was carried out under Pope Paul V. When he became pope in 1605, he ordered the destruction of the remaining parts of the old Constantinian building that were still standing and two years later held a competition for the design of the facade. It was won by Carlo Maderno, who was then Architect of St. Peter's. Maderno extended the eastern arm of Michelangelo's centrally planned church, creating a long nave, and in 1612 added a facade that stretched across a front much wider than the body of the church.

The final building's scale is awe-inspiring: the length of the nave from the entrance to the Chair of St. Peter in the apse is 615 feet (187 m) and the width across the transepts is 450 feet (137 m). The great English Gothic cathedral at Salisbury could be placed inside St. Peter's, and its spire, the tallest in England, would not touch the top of the 434-foot (132-m) dome.

The effect of Maderno's alterations on Michelangelo's work has been much criticized, particularly since, from the east, at less than a quarter of a mile, the facade obscures Michelangelo's dome. But Maderno's long nave, echoing that of the original basilica, is more appropriate than that of Michelangelo for processional ceremonial.

In 1629, Gianlorenzo Bernini, then age 31, became Architect of St. Peter's. One of the greatest artistic geniuses of the seventeenth century, he had already achieved considerable public success as a sculptor at the age of just 19. Socially he was charming, witty, and convivial, as well as fashionable and elegant. Professionally he was a great organizer, working creatively with amazing rapidity, and his impact on the visual character of the cathedral was as powerful as Michelangelo's.

Bernini designed the *baldacchino*, or canopy, which rises above the papal altar under the

One of the great curving arms of the elliptical piazza's free-standing colonnade masks the facade of St. Peter's in this unusual view. The colonnade's 228 pillars, each 60 feet (18 m) high, are banked four deep and, on the piazza front, are topped by sculpted figures more than 10 feet (3 m) high. The piazza was completed in 1667.

dome. He created the extravagant Chair of St. Peter in the apse, which is best viewed framed by the columns of the *baldacchino*. And he transformed an undefined, unrelated space in front of the cathedral by constructing the great piazza, whose central point is the ancient Egyptian obelisk which was erected in front of St. Peter's in 1586. Furthermore, he completed several sculpted tombs and figures in the church.

Although the majesty of St. Peter's owes most to Michelangelo, Bernini's work invests the grandeur of the building with something of the mystery, awe, energy, and dominance of the Roman Church in the seventeenth century, and it may be that his contributions have the deepest impact on the emotions.

Monticello, Virginia

"I am as happy nowhere else, and in no other society, and all my wishes end, where I hope my days will end, at Monticello."

THESE WORDS OF THOMAS JEFFERSON, THE owner, architect, designer, and master builder of the house he named Monticello, expressed his passionate attachment to the home he built, altered, and rebuilt over a period of 40 years. His hope was fulfilled, for he died there on July 4, 1826, the 50th anniversary of the signing of the Declaration of Independence, which he had drafted at Monticello.

For Jefferson was much more than a land-owner and architect. He was born on April 13, 1743, at Shadwell, his family's large estate in Albemarle County, Virginia, where he grew up. At the age of 24, he received 5,000 acres (2,025 ha) from his father's estate and in 1770 moved into the small bachelor house he had built at Monticello, the site where he was to mastermind the realization of his architectural dream – the house that stands today.

Jefferson's early career was as a successful lawyer in Virginia, but his ambition and abilities extended to the wider field of politics, which included for him a deep concern for the future of the American community (at that time the American colonies, of which Virginia was the first, were still administered by the British parliament). In 1768, the year before Jefferson began building at Monticello, he was elected to the House of Burgesses and, importantly, joined the revolutionary group.

He was instrumental in the formation of the 1774 Continental Congress, and a delegate to it as well, which led to his drafting the Declaration of Independence in 1776. In 1779 he became Governor of Virginia and five years later was sent to France as a pleni-potentiary. In 1789, he was recalled to

THE DIGNIFIED CLASSICISM of the exterior of Monticello was enhanced by the pleasing proportions of Jefferson's designs for the balustrade and entablatures and his attention to detail – he even specified the size of the bricks, 7½ x 2½ inches (19 x 6.4 cm). This care was also evident in the interior cornices and door moldings, the parlor's cherry and beech parquet floor, and in the effort he made to find the exact shade of green paint for the hall floor. Elsewhere are many examples of his unconventional solutions to common problems.

Jefferson was a great advocate of light and air and favored octagonal rooms that created a semicircle he could fill with windows; in the dining room and his bedroom, each of which had only one window, he introduced skylights as well.

Two dumb-waiters in the ends of the dining room mantelpiece were used to bring up bottles from the wine cellar below.

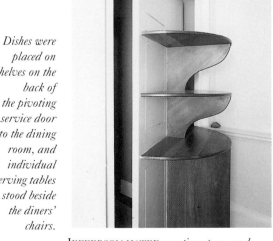

Dishes were placed on shelves on the back of the pivoting service door to the dining room, and individual serving tables stood beside the diners' chairs.

JEFFERSON HATED *wasting space, and his ingenuity in devising ways to use it is clearly shown in the dining room. There was, however, another reason for the self-service devices he installed: his intense dislike of servants intruding upon his privacy and reducing the "free and unrestricted flow of conversation."*

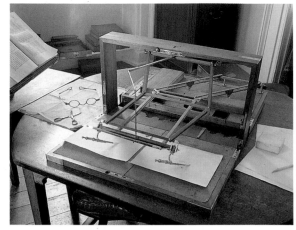

THE PANTOGRAPH *(above)* was used after 1779 by Jefferson – a prolific letter writer – to make file copies of letters and important documents. A second pen attached to the device made a copy as he wrote.

Also in the study was Jefferson's adjustable table. Metal legs slid out of the wooden ones, allowing the top to be raised. It could also be tilted to any angle to form the drawing board on which he made most of his plans and sketches for Monticello and, later, the University of Virginia at Charlottesville nearby. As work progressed there, he could observe it by telescope from Monticello.

Washington, and after a further three-year period he retired from public life to his beloved Monticello, where he continued his building program. But such was Jefferson's reputation as an administrator and a brilliant mind that after two years he was persuaded to become Vice President of the United States; in 1801 he became its third president, serving for two terms until 1809. By this time, he had managed to finish the major work on Monticello, although he continued to make minor adjustments for the rest of his life.

That such a busy and important career could have allowed the continuation of work on his house is surprising enough, but when we realize that he made most of the measured drawings for every detail, down to scale drawings for parts of sash windows, it becomes entirely astonishing. A single example serves to show the care and ability that was characteristic of all Jefferson's activities. In 1803, when he was completing the Louisiana Purchase, the largest purchase of land in history, he made a full-size drawing, one of many, for the "Frize and Cornice for the inner window of the Dining room," adding the note, "A 7 to 1 architrave having been put by mistake instead of one of $8\frac{1}{2}$ to 1, the frize and cornice must be proportioned to the 7 to 1."

Jefferson has been described as the greatest native-born architect of his time in America. In addition to Monticello, he designed, built, and, in some instances, supervised the construction of at least six houses, a church, the State Capitol in Richmond, the new capital of Virginia, and the greatest of all university complexes, at Charlottesville in Virginia. He also produced a number of designs that remained unbuilt, including a Governor's House for Virginia and a prison.

One of his final designs was for his own tombstone on which was cut his epitaph for himself: "Here was buried Thomas Jefferson, Author of the Declaration of American Independence, of the Statute of Virginia for Religious Freedom, and Father of the University of Virginia." No mention was made of the Presidency and other important achievements.

Jefferson was entirely self-trained and seems not to have had any early passion for architecture, although he had seen a number of books on the subject in the library of

JEFFERSON'S PORTRAIT *was painted by Thomas Sully at Monticello in 1821, when he was at last able to spend time with his family and to indulge his passions: for mathematics, the classics, architecture, "putting up and pulling down," and, increasingly, gardening.*

PALLADIO'S INFLUENCE *is evident in the first design for Monticello, which is based on the Villa Pisani. It has a dominant, pedimented portico on the second story, but ignores Palladio's rule that the space between the columns defining the entrance should be wider than that on either side. The use of Roman Doric and Ionic orders is typical.*

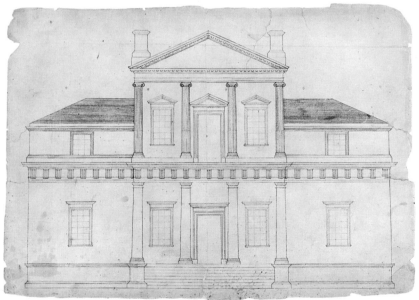

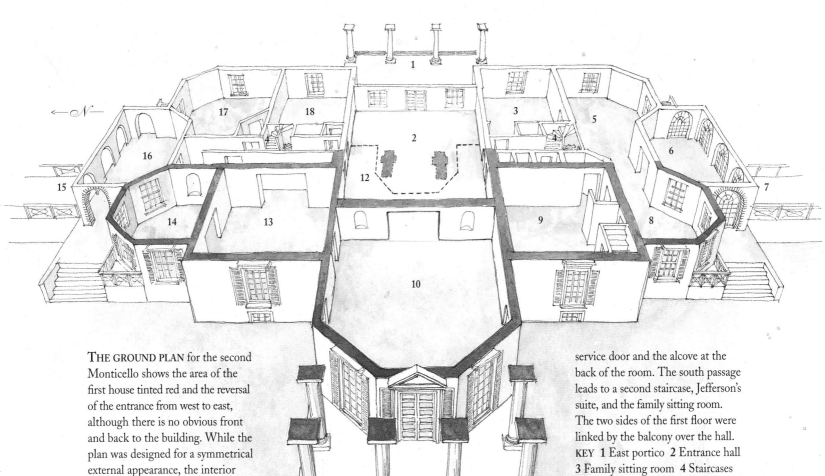

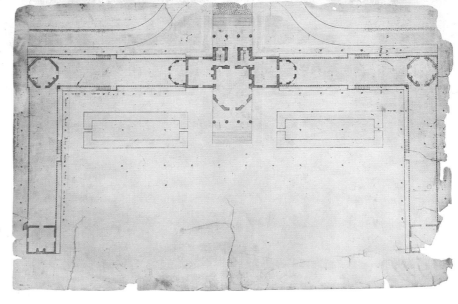

THE GROUND PLAN for the second Monticello shows the area of the first house tinted red and the reversal of the entrance from west to east, although there is no obvious front and back to the building. While the plan was designed for a symmetrical external appearance, the interior shows that the layout of the original house was not simply repeated in the second one, but that there was a variety of arrangements.

Narrow passageways leading off the hall give access on the north to a staircase, the guest bedrooms, and the dining room, via the pivoting service door and the alcove at the back of the room. The south passage leads to a second staircase, Jefferson's suite, and the family sitting room. The two sides of the first floor were linked by the balcony over the hall.

KEY **1** East portico **2** Entrance hall **3** Family sitting room **4** Staircases **5** Library **6** Conservatory **7** South terrace **8** Jefferson's cabinet **9** Jefferson's bedroom **10** Parlor **11** West portico **12** Balcony **13** Dining room **14** Tea room **15** North terrace **16** North piazza **17** and **18** Guest bedrooms

A PERIOD *in Paris (1784–89) gave Jefferson first-hand experience of trends in European architecture. Perhaps the structure that most influenced the final form of Monticello was the dome on an octagonal drum. The spacious, well-lit dome room – "a noble and beautiful apartment," according to one visitor – with its pivoting windows that afforded a vista of the surrounding countryside, was intended as a billiard room, but was never used except, later, for storage.*

JEFFERSON'S DEBT *to Palladio can be seen in the plan for the first Monticello, showing the terrace wings and terminal pavilions. The octagonal corner pavilions were not built, but the terminal pavilions were, and they were retained for the second house. The roofs of the wings were tiled and these terraces, as they were known, were finished with a wooden balustrade made to a pattern shown in Sir William Chambers's book of 1757,* Designs of Chinese Buildings.

William Byrd II, whose home, Westover, was the only house in the region to show a knowledge of design. Byrd's library contained a number of architectural volumes that probably sparked some interest in Jefferson. From his college days, architecture was a developing concern for him, and, since there were no architectural schools, he was committed to self-education through books, and created one of the finest libraries in America.

The first book he owned on architecture was probably Andrea Palladio's *The Four Books of Architecture*, first published in English in 1715. Since the sixteenth century, Palladio had been an important influence in European architecture, and to him Jefferson accorded his lifelong allegiance. Directly and indirectly, Palladio's influence infused all Jefferson's buildings, and both houses at Monticello showed his impact in their design.

Most colonial houses, even Jefferson's early home Shadwell, were of wooden cottage form, made by craftsmen whose familiarity with any architectural style was rudimentary. Such architectural elements as were present were usually crudely made and stuck on for some undefined effect. It is difficult to overestimate the refinement of detail which Jefferson introduced, for he set a standard of finish and accuracy not known in America at the time.

Monticello was built on land that Jefferson had known and loved from childhood, and his decision to build his house there was not surprising; the surprise lay in his choice of a site. For obvious practical reasons, most houses in undeveloped countryside were built on low-lying ground near a river or stream; Jefferson sited his house on a hill, with a wide view all around and an outlook to the Blue Ridge Mountains in the west. In 1767, he wrote the word "Hermitage" in his garden book, then crossed it out and wrote "Monticello," Italian for little mountain. From this time, he was constantly planning, but work did not begin until two years later.

The inspiration for the first house stems in particular from Palladio's design for the two-story Villa Pisani, near Padua, with a double portico, and from a design in *The Four Books* that shows a house with two connected, enclosing arms. The winged-villa form was an important part of the first plan for Monticello which was retained in the final house,

THE DINING ROOM, *part of the original building that was retained in the second house, is one of the most attractive rooms. Here Jefferson entertained his friends with good food, fine French and Italian wines, and intelligent conversation.*

His innovations included the first use in America of "double glazing" to insulate the room from the winter cold. There were double sashes on the window and double sliding doors into the north-facing tea room, where the family breakfasted.

ALL THE BEDS *in the house were set in alcoves, leaving the bedrooms free for daytime use, but Jefferson made special arrangements for himself. His bed was set between two rooms and was accessible either from his cabinet, or study, or from his bedroom, which was mainly used as a dressing room and was lit by a skylight. The bed could be raised during the day to allow free passage between the two rooms. Three porthole windows in the wall above the bed admitted air and light to a clothes closet, reached by a ladder, while Jefferson's daily clothes were hung on a clothes tree in an alcove at the foot of the bed.*

THE ENTRANCE HALL *on the east of the house led directly to the parlor. Since it was two stories high, a balcony (from which this picture was taken) was needed to link the two halves of the first floor. The hall contained many interesting features and was filled with Native American artifacts, natural history specimens, and other curios.*

The most unusual object was the seven-day calendar clock above the main entrance. It had two faces: an internal one, showing the hours, minutes, and seconds, and an external one under the portico with

only an hour hand and a gong, which sounded on the hour for the benefit of estate workers and house servants.

As the cannonball weights descended, they passed black bars on the right-hand wall, indicating the days of the week. Holes in the floor allowed the weights to descend into the basement, where Saturday's mark was located.

Among items designed by Jefferson were the ladder, which was used to wind the clock and could be folded into a single plank, and 28 black-painted "stick chairs," made by cabinetmakers on the estate.

although, characteristically, Jefferson used the idea in a personal manner. He half-sank the wings into the slope of the hill to form a semi-basement so that his view was not obscured, and placed in them all the service rooms (or, as he called them, dependencies). These included the kitchen, wine and beer cellars, storerooms, stables, and servants' quarters. At the end of each of the two wings was a small pavilion, the one on the south being his original small bachelor house, which gives a clear indication that the overall design was in his mind from the beginning.

Little of the first house remains in the second, very different, structure, for in 1796 Jefferson embarked on an extensive "re-edification," or remodeling. This was meant to be finished quickly: "I have begun the demolition of my house and hope to get through its re-edification in the course of the summer," he wrote. But the following year, he became vice president, and duty took him away from Monticello.

Jefferson's decision to alter the house was inspired primarily by the period he spent in France and by a visit he made to England. In Paris, he particularly liked the Hôtel de Salm, then being built, which was surmounted by a dome, and in England he visited Lord Burlington's domed villa at Chiswick, near London, which was based on Palladio's Villa Rotonda just outside Vicenza. The dome was for Jefferson a new and exciting architectural element, which at Monticello became a dominant feature.

The final, 21-room house was on three floors above the semi-basement, but Jefferson employed much ingenuity to make it appear externally as if it were on only one. On the east side, the height of the columns on the portico and the linking of the ground-floor windows with those of the bedrooms above helped to achieve this effect. On the second floor the dome room was hidden behind the balustrade running around the house, and the windows of the three attic bedrooms were incorporated into the frieze beneath the balustrade.

AN AERIAL VIEW *of the house and surrounding gardens, with the wide Virginia landscape behind, shows how Jefferson used the commanding site to full effect. The lawns and serpentine walk, together with the mature trees and woodlands, provided an idyllic setting for the civilized lifestyle that Jefferson desired and enjoyed.*

Internally, creating an intriguing spatial effect in an otherwise symmetrical plan, ceiling heights on the ground floor varied between about 18 feet (5.5 m) in the hall, dining room, tea room, parlor, and Jefferson's bedroom, and some 10–11 feet (3–3.4 m) in the other rooms.

Another notable feature was the apparent absence of a staircase. In most large houses, staircases are a strong visual feature, but Jefferson thought them a waste of space "which would make a good room in every story," so he hid them in the thickness of partition walls and made them steep and narrow.

The great modern American architect Frank Lloyd Wright once observed that designing a house is like painting a portrait, and this can never have been more true than of Jefferson and Monticello. It is the embodiment of his developing understanding of architecture, his inventive mind, his personal, unconventional style, and his highly civilized nature.

BUCKINGHAM PALACE, LONDON

"If the Public wish to have a Palace I have no objection to build one...I will have it at Buckingham House..."

KING GEORGE IV'S DECISION INITIATED A process that led to the transformation of a grand private house into the new official residence of an old monarchy. As George himself said, he had enjoyed many hours of pleasure in the Duke of Buckingham's house, which his father George III had bought as a private residence and into which he had moved with Queen Charlotte in 1763.

The 40 acres (16 ha) of land on which Buckingham House was built had been obtained by the Crown in the sixteenth century. Most of it had been leased out, but on the remaining 4 acres (1.6 ha) James I had, in the early 1600s, created a Mulberry Garden in which thousands of mulberry trees had been planted to encourage a silk industry to rival that of the French. The project failed, and the ground was leased to Lord Goring; upon his death, the lease was taken over by Lord Arlington, who built an imposing house on the site. In 1702, the first Duke of Buckingham acquired the lease, pulled down the existing Arlington House, and began building his own mansion.

Buckingham House was built on a grand scale; it was a splendid mansion of brick and stone, designed by William Winde in Dutch Palladian style, with a central block and a wing on each side, joined by a colonnade (*see illustration left*). An attempt in 1760 by the duke's heir, Sir Charles Sheffield, to renew the lease of the entire area failed, and in 1762 George III was able to buy the mansion, with the intention of providing a home for his 19-year-old queen should he die before her. It became known as The Queen's House.

Tʜᴇ ꜰᴀᴄᴀᴅᴇ of Buckingham Palace facing the Mall – the one it offers to the public – is a rather bland, Classical screen hiding the more lively architecture of John Nash's courtyard front behind its flat, gray-white Portland stone.

The plain exterior does not reflect the splendor of the interiors, such as those on the garden front, shown here. The White and Blue Drawing Rooms and the Music Room, with elaborate molded and gilded plasterwork ceilings and columns painted to resemble onyx or lapis lazuli, are among Nash's most ornate designs. The patterns on the specially made carpets in the drawing rooms harmonize with the ceilings, and all the rooms contain magnificent furniture, chandeliers, paintings, clocks, and Sèvres porcelain.

Tʜᴇ ᴅɪssᴏʟᴜᴛᴇ *and spendthrift Prince of Wales (Prince Regent from 1811) became King George IV in 1820. This detail, from a full-length portrait by Sir Thomas Lawrence, shows the king in his coronation robes (which cost £24,000). It now hangs in the State Dining Room.*

Qᴜᴇᴇɴ Vɪᴄᴛᴏʀɪᴀ, *the first monarch to live in the palace, was painted with seven of her nine children by a well-known artist of the period, John Callcott Horsley. Prince* Edward holds a plan of the Crystal Palace, designed by Joseph Paxton for the Great Exhibition of 1851, while the building itself is pictured in the distance.

NASH CONVERTED *Queen Charlotte's living quarters in the original Queen's House into a picture gallery.*

The present appearance of the gallery, which is the largest room in the palace, was the result of alterations made by Edward Blore in the late 1830s and, finally, of changes made by Sir Aston Webb in 1913.

In order to create a well-lit and uncluttered space, Webb installed the curved glass ceiling and removed a double-columned alcove at the far end of the room, as well as several large gilded chandeliers.

THE GRAND STAIRCASE, *which opens off the Grand Hall, was designed by Nash. It is an elaborate gilded and balustraded structure that divides into three flights at the first landing. Two companion flights, one of which is shown here, curve* up to the Guard Room; the third leads directly to the East Gallery. The portraits include George III, Queen Charlotte, and William IV; the statue at the top of the stairs is a copy of Benvenuto Cellini's bronze, Perseus with the Head of Medusa.

George III enlarged the house and employed Sir William Chambers, an important architect, to modernize the interior to provide accommodations for the royal family as well as for the vast collection of works of art and books he was to accumulate during his long life. (After his death, it was discovered that he had also kept all his clothing.) The effect of the enlargement was to change a rectangular forecourt into a dignified, if slightly old-fashioned, arrangement.

On the death of George III in 1820, his son, who had been Prince Regent since 1811 during the king's final period of madness, became King George IV, at the age of 58. He had had a separate establishment in Buckingham House since 1781, and part at least of the affection he had for Buckingham House stemmed from the extravagant lifestyle he had enjoyed while living there.

Sometimes praised as "the first gentleman of Europe," George IV was also often seen in a less flattering light. Charles Greville, who knew him well, considered that "a more contemptible, cowardly, unfeeling selfish dog does not exist"; another view was that he was "a bad son, a bad husband, a bad father, a bad subject, a bad monarch and a bad friend." In the light of these opinions, it is surprising to learn of the considerable energy and imagination that he showed in the creation of architectural projects in London.

During his regency, with his favorite architect John Nash, he planned the development of Regent's Park, the rows of grand houses around it, Regent Street, and Carlton House Terrace. When his mother died in 1818, he began replanning The Queen's House, which, at his instigation, again became Buckingham House. On his accession, it became a great passion and one of his major projects. But initial governmental refusal to finance the work adequately and the many changes to Nash's plans demanded by the king meant work did not start until 1825.

Buckingham House was an almost impossible problem for Nash. The king was a difficult master, parliament was not generous in voting the necessary money, and Nash had to adapt an already existing structure for a very different use. His solution was to enlarge the main house and the two great arms on the eastern side to create an enclosing forecourt

JOHN NASH'S *portrait, painted in 1827 by Sir Thomas Lawrence, shows him as the successful businessman he finally became. But Nash's staid looks belie his temperament: he was "clever, impetuous, vivacious… better at conceiving big ideas than at carrying them out in detail" – characteristics he shared with his royal patron. Nash produced some of the most imaginative architecture of the period in styles ranging from Classical to "Oriental" – seen in the Brighton Pavilion – and Neogothic, which he used in his own home, East Cowes Castle on the Isle of Wight.*

THE CENTER ROOM, *on the eastern front, opens onto the balcony on which the royal family appears to greet the crowds that gather in the Mall and around the Victoria Memorial, seen here through the* door. The millions who have gazed up at the royal family must have wondered what the room behind them holds. Decorated in Chinese style, it features *chinoiserie fireplaces from the Brighton Pavilion.*

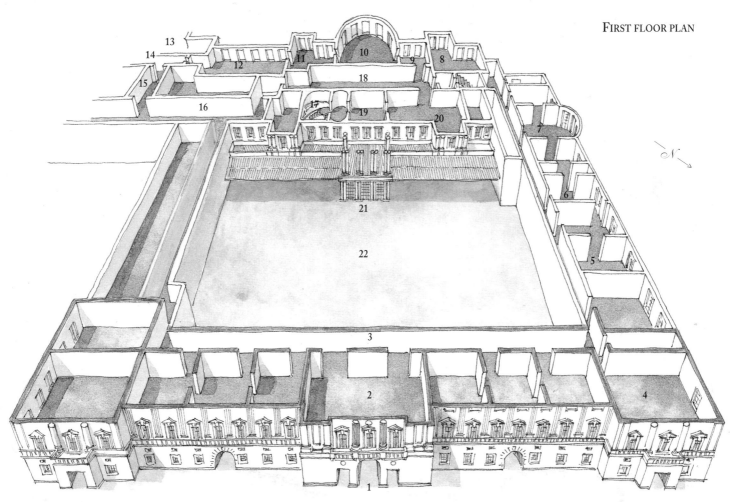

SWEEPING LAWNS, *flowerbeds, and a pond with flamingos form a fitting setting for Nash's garden front, seen only by privileged visitors. The warm ochre Bath stone contrasts pleasantly with the gray-white Portland stone of the east front seen from the Mall. The central bow and dome, which dominate the composition, form the central part of the Bow Room and, above it, the Music Room.*

THE PLAN shows most of the state rooms, which are located on the west side of the quadrangle and are approached via the Grand Hall and Grand Staircase, both by Nash. The screen building facing the Mall, which was added by Blore, is tinted red.

KEY 1 Mall entrance 2 Center Room 3 Principal Corridor 4 Chinese Dining Room

5 Prince Philip's suite 6 The Queen's bedroom suite 7 The Queen's study 8 Audience Chamber 9 White Drawing Room 10 Music Room 11 Blue Drawing Room 12 State Dining Room 13 Ballroom 14 West Gallery 15 Cross Gallery 16 East Gallery 17 Grand Staircase and Grand Hall 18 Picture Gallery 19 Green Drawing Room 20 Throne Room 21 Nash forecourt front 22 Quadrangle

facing the Mall, in front of which he erected the Marble Arch. The western, garden, side he redesigned to introduce a central bow and dome. Conservatories at either end were connected by a broad stone terrace running the full length of the building. This facade is the only external work by Nash that remains substantially unchanged, but he had completed the decoration of many of the rooms by 1830, when, after the death of George IV, he was dismissed and accused of many malpractices.

During the seven-year reign of William IV, the younger brother of George IV, work continued; but although William had been born in Buckingham House, he showed little interest in the building program. When he died in 1837, the palace had been ready for occupation for a month. He was succeeded by his niece Victoria, the daughter of his brother Edward, who became the first monarch to live in Buckingham Palace.

Victoria moved into the palace only three weeks after her accession and had a profound influence on its final form, since, from the beginning of her reign, she considered it too small and not suitable for family life and state functions. In 1840 she married Prince Albert of Saxe-Coburg and Gotha. He was a much more experienced and educated figure than his young wife, and his influence was added to Victoria's in realizing plans for the extension of the palace. The couple had nine children, four boys and five girls, and this growing family increased the urgency for the completion of the work in the 1840s and '50s.

The importance of Victoria's long reign of 64 years should not be overlooked in determining the effect of the royal palace on the public. The Victorian age established the monarchy, produced stability in government, and created a worldwide empire. On the domestic scene, it transformed the country into an industrial power, with all the benefits and problems that such developments bring. Victoria, as she aged, became the autocratic mother of the nation, and as her main home and the center of ceremony, Buckingham Palace became the symbol of that authority, power, and stability; and so it has remained.

Architecturally, the finished palace is a mixture of unresolved intentions and ill-fitting parts. An article in the August 1847

A DELIGHTFUL ROOM, *the Green Drawing Room, decorated in various shades of green with gilt details, was Queen Charlotte's Saloon before Nash redesigned it. The chairs in green silk, made in the 1820s, were originally intended for Windsor Castle.*

THE AUDIENCE ROOM *overlooks the gardens on the west front and is part of Queen Elizabeth II's private suite on the first floor. It is a light, airy room, used by the queen for informal or private meetings with officials and members of the government.*

NASH'S PLAN *for the State Dining Room was amended between 1831and 1840 by Edward Blore. The handsome plasterwork ceiling he designed has three saucer domes and a deep, coved cornice decorated with foliage and flowers. On the walls hang portraits of George IV and all the earlier Hanoverian kings.*

issue of the magazine *The Builder* states that "the design does not pretend to grandeur or magnificence, scarcely to dignity." One of the problems was the absence of distinguished architects. Edward Blore, who followed Nash, undertook the first architectural projects for Queen Victoria. A fairly competent designer, he proposed a dramatic solution to the need for more living space. Across the forecourt that fronted Nash's Classical composition for the east side, Blore placed a five-story screen building, which required the removal of the Marble Arch to Hyde Park. The effect was to isolate the facade seen by the public from the architecture of the forecourt front and the west, garden, side.

On the first floor, the screen front contains the 80-yard (73-m) long Principal Corridor, linking the Household Corridor on the south with the Royal Corridor on the north; some state rooms, including the Center Room, open off it and face east onto St. James's Park and along the Mall. In 1852, Sir James Pennethorne, Nash's student and also his adopted son – he may, in fact, have been George IV's illegitimate son – added a ballroom and supper room on the southwestern corner of the palace.

The facade of Buckingham Palace seen from St. James's Park, with its Classical pillars and pediment, is strongly reminiscent of the Villa Pisani at Stra, in Italy, built in the 18th century.

Blore's east front was completed in 1847, but it is not the facade that is seen today. In 1913, Sir Aston Webb – a well-known architect who was also responsible for the Victoria Memorial, the Admiralty Arch at the far end of the Mall, and the Victoria and Albert Museum – was employed to reface Blore's ornate and already deteriorating facade with a more clearly Classical design in Portland stone, a sharp gray-white contrast to the Bath stone used by Nash and Blore.

If any building establishes the thesis of this book – that really to know any building it is necessary to penetrate the facade – it is Buckingham Palace, for the disappointingly unimpressive exterior is in sharp contrast to the interior, which exhibits a large-scale, sumptuous magnificence in all the state rooms as well as in many of the private apartments. Much of the interior still reveals the brilliance of Nash's imagination, modified by the needs of Queen Victoria and the taste of the Prince Consort. Although many changes have taken place since Victoria died, the palace continues to bear the imprint of her dominant personality and the glories of the days of British imperial power.

The palace has been a royal residence for less than 200 years, but it has remained one of the most revered of all royal homes. Since World War I, it has become a symbol of national unity, drawing enthusiastic crowds, who assemble in front of the building to express their loyalty to the monarch at times of national crisis or to share with the royal family in rejoicing.

The Opéra Garnier, Paris

"As a matter of fact, the whole trend in Paris is now toward the colossal. Everything is becoming wild and out of proportion."

In 1867, when Gustave Flaubert made this comment in a letter to George Sand, he was writing about a Paris in the throes of a disruptive metamorphosis greater than has occurred in any other modern city. In the course of a decade, it changed from a medieval town, with a warren of unhealthy and dangerous narrow streets that were full of cutthroats, pickpockets, hawkers, prostitutes, and entertainers, into a clearly planned city, with broad tree-lined boulevards in a radical layout with clear nodal points.

This was achieved only by the great determination of two men: Emperor Napoleon III and the Prefect of the Department of the Seine, Baron Haussmann. Napoleon had three principal objectives for Paris: to make it a suitably magnificent imperial capital, a secure seat of government against violent insurrection, and a city adapted to the needs of a growing population and expanding industry.

Nothing had previously been attempted on this scale. Under Haussmann, Paris acquired 90 miles (145 km) of new streets, 354 miles (570 km) of underground sewers, 4,400 acres (1,780 ha) of new parks, including the Bois de Boulogne, and hundreds of new public and private buildings. Flaubert's sensitive nature was appalled by the vulgarity and display that often accompanied these works, including the Paris Opera (now known as the Opéra Garnier), the exterior of which was almost finished when he wrote to George Sand.

Haussmann's remodeling followed about 70 years of violent upheaval in France. The dramatic impact of the French Revolution and the reign of Emperor Napoleon I had

THE FACADE (*previous page*) is best viewed from the Avenue de l'Opéra and from some distance, when the relationship of the three elements of vestibules and foyer, auditorium, and stage and backstage area can be most clearly seen.

But Garnier's genius both as designer and architect is evident in the Stair Hall. The Grand Staircase, rising from the pavilions to the auditorium, is a theatrical triumph. It creates a sense of well-being, anticipation, and delight in all theater-goers, for whom pleasure and indulgence go hand in hand. It covers an area almost as large as the auditorium, indicating the importance Garnier attached to its psychological effect.

THE ENTIRE BUILDING *was designed to express levels of privilege, and the grandest entrance was naturally reserved for the emperor. It is fronted by a double curved ramp leading to a porte-cochère where passengers could alight from their carriages under cover.*

EXTENDING ACROSS THE *width of the Opéra, the foyer is the most sumptuous elaboration of the Baroque in the whole interior. Huge chandeliers illuminate the rich gilt decoration of the vaulted hall, with its rows of double columns echoing those on the facade.*

THE DANCE, *a copy of which adorns the facade of the Opéra, was Carpeaux's masterpiece. Full of life and urgency, the sculpture shows an exuberance that establishes his position as the artistic forerunner of Rodin.*

LITTLE ARTISTIC *quality characterizes Paul Baudry's strongly colored ceiling panels in the foyer (detail below). They do, however, provide a lively addition to the richness of the foyer's overall decoration.*

changed the character of French society beyond all recognition. Then in 1848 – known in Europe as the Year of Revolutions – King Louis Philippe abdicated and the Second French Republic was declared. Napoleon I's nephew, Louis Napoleon, was elected president of the Republic. In 1852, after a remarkably modern, highly organized and stage-managed coup d'état, the president declared himself Emperor Napoleon III and embarked upon his ambitious plans.

Five years later, an assassination attempt was made on the emperor while he was on his way to a theater. This event accelerated work on clearing the narrow and dangerous streets in the center of Paris and opening up the area around the many theaters (in the nineteenth century Paris had more theaters than any other European city). As part of this cleanup, the old opera house in the Rue de Peletier was marked for demolition. Plans were made for a new building – officially called the Académie Nationale de Musique, but always known as the Opéra – to be erected in the center of the nearby Place de l'Opéra as a venue for opera, ballet, and concerts.

A competition was held, and 171 entries were submitted. A design by the young architect Charles Garnier, just 35 years old, was placed fifth, admitting him to the final stage of the competition, which he won. His design for what was to become the Opéra Garnier has been called the finest design of its period and the identifying structure of the Second Empire style. The Opéra received many accolades and also much criticism, one English observer describing it as "an overloaded sideboard." Having expected the commission to go to her favorite architect, the famous Viollet-le-Duc, the Empress Eugénie did not like the building on principle; when she asked what style it was, Garnier replied, diplomatically but accurately, that it was the style of Napoleon III.

Despite adverse criticism, since its opening in January 1875, the Opéra has been hugely popular. It is, in fact, an extraordinary architectural achievement, astonishing for a young and inexperienced architect. The lucidity and clarity of the design and its appropriateness to the purpose, the coherence between form and decoration, and the physical grandeur all come together stunningly.

THE PLAN of the Opéra suits its purpose perfectly, as is revealed in this cross-section. Almost half the building is designed for public activities. Seven doorways in the facade provide access for the general public; there are separate entrances, located on the left and right sides, for dignitaries and season-ticket holders. These entrances have access to special refreshment pavilions; the one for season-ticket holders can be seen here beneath the auditorium.

Theatergoers move from the entrances to the Stair Hall and up the stunning Grand Staircase – Garnier's pièce de résistance – to the auditorium level, where the main vestibule, the sumptuous foyer, and the balconies and corridors for promenading are located. The central area taken up by the auditorium is relatively small, while the huge stage and fly-space, backstage area, and administrative offices constitute the rest of the building.

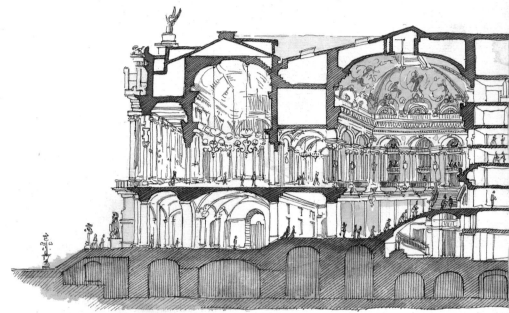

A BRONZE BUST of Garnier, modeled in 1869 by his friend and collaborator Jean-Baptiste Carpeaux, reflects the nervous sensitivity of both sitter and artist. A copy of this work was used for the monument to Garnier that was erected at the side of the Opéra in 1903.

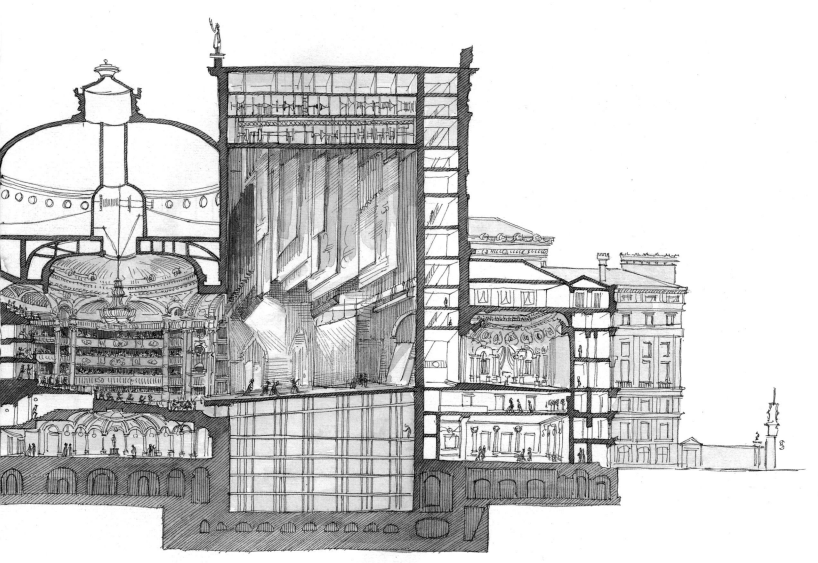

CROSS-SECTION AND GROUND PLAN

The clarity of Garnier's composition is evident in both the ground plan and the cross-section through the central axis. The three main elements: the public areas, the auditorium, and the stage and production areas are clearly distinguished. At the center is the auditorium, which provides the focus of the design, while the horseshoe shape directs attention toward the stage and the various areas of activity that lie behind it: sets, storage, rehearsal areas, dressing rooms, and administrative offices. Almost half the building is devoted to these practical matters. The ground plan, in particular, reveals the strongly rectilinear basis for the design and Garnier's extremely successful use of the diamond-shaped site – a jewel within a jewel.

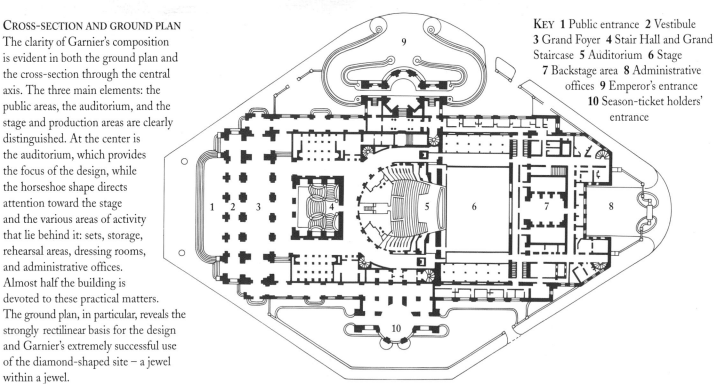

KEY **1** Public entrance **2** Vestibule **3** Grand Foyer **4** Stair Hall and Grand Staircase **5** Auditorium **6** Stage **7** Backstage area **8** Administrative offices **9** Emperor's entrance **10** Season-ticket holders' entrance

The grand building was a fitting symbol for the beau monde, the new society of financiers and industrialists – full of energy, some majesty, and vulgarity – that had replaced the old pre-revolution aristocracy. A wonderful, unique monument, Garnier's masterpiece was, and remains today, a focal point of Paris. Sometimes jokingly called the Palais Garnier, it is now, since the building of a new opera house at the Bastille, officially known as the Opéra Garnier. This is a final, just recognition of the scale of Garnier's achievement.

Jean-Louis-Charles Garnier (1825–98) was of humble origins, the son of a blacksmith in a notorious part of Paris. Too frail to work the smithy bellows and showing some talent in drawing, he was placed in a drawing school, where he met his lifelong friend, the sculptor Jean-Baptiste Carpeaux. At the age of 17, Garnier was admitted to the Ecole des Beaux Arts and, at the same time, worked as an architectural draftsman to support himself.

Soon he began to achieve some distinction, winning the Grand Prix de Rome. He spent the years from 1848 to 1854 in Rome, where the great balls and pageants fired his imagination and helped develop his decorative sensibility. On a visit to Greece during this time, he met the writer Théophile Gautier, who became his friend and ardent supporter.

On his return from Rome, Garnier worked in local government offices until, in 1860, the competition for the Opéra changed his life. For the next 15 years, the project became his main preoccupation – he designed every aspect of the building and also supervised the construction. Building began in August 1861, the foundation stone was laid in July of the following year, and the exterior was more or less completed by August 1867.

But the interior was not finished, and construction was suspended during the Franco–Prussian War of 1870–71. While Paris was occupied by the German army, the shell of the building was used as a hospital, a warehouse, a barracks, and a fort. In 1873, the old opera house, then still in use, was destroyed by fire, and work on the new building was accelerated until its official opening in January 1875. Regrettably, Napoleon III died in 1873 and neither saw his great enterprise open nor entered the theater he had done so much to bring into being.

LITTLE HAS ALTERED *in the auditorium (right) since the first performance. The main change is Marc Chagall's ceiling, commissioned in 1964. The proposal aroused such opposition that a false ceiling was installed; on it, in five differently colored zones, Chagall painted scenes dedicated to great composers for opera and ballet, including Mozart and Tchaikovsky.*

THE ELABORATE STAIRCASE *rises through three levels: from the access on the lowest level for season-ticket holders, to the raised entrance floor reached from the foyer, and then to the auditorium. In this unusual view, the star-shaped, multicolored inlay in the marble floor on the lowest level is just visible.*

A SYMBOLIC MASK, *possibly of Thor, is among many decorative details on the main staircase. Most of the designs for the craftsmen-sculptors were provided by Garnier, and one observer noted that no one before had drawn ornament as freely and expressively.*

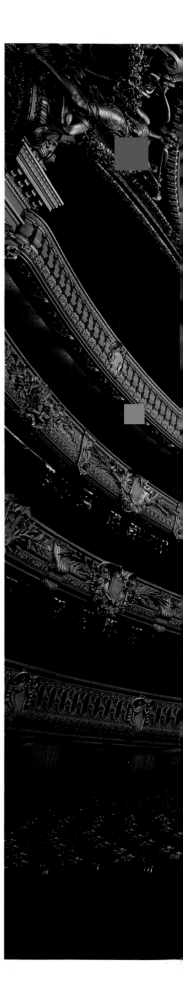

The building is composed of three main elements: first, the foyer, vestibules, and Stair Hall; second, the central auditorium; and third, the stage and dressing rooms. These elements can be clearly identified externally, and they are integrated internally in a smoothly flowing design. The horseshoe-shaped auditorium, with four tiers of boxes, can seat some 2,000 people. It is surmounted by a half-dome elevated on a drum, and originally there was a false, shallow internal dome that created an almost spherical interior. The auditorium dome is flanked externally by two smaller domes, each above a side entrance, the one for holders of season tickets, the other, with a double sweeping ramp leading to a porte-cochère, the emperor's entrance. Perhaps because Napoleon III had died and because the Franco–Prussian War was followed by the Third Republic, this entrance was never finished.

Behind the half-dome of the auditorium, and framing it, rises the rectangular pedimented form of the stage, dressing rooms, and fly-space, which contains the mechanism for raising and lowering the scenery. The pediment is topped by a statue of Apollo, the god of music, holding aloft a lyre. The different functions of the auditorium and the stage are clearly indicated in Garnier's composition. The same is true of the main entrance, through seven large arched doorways, into the vestibule, which in turn opens into the Stair Hall with its Grand Staircase.

This is the most original, elaborately decorated and dramatic element in the whole design. The use of richly veined marble, gilt decorative balustrades, and bronze and marble figures holding bright candelabra gives a sense of sumptuous indulgence, which makes the staircase the place in which to see and be seen. The whole public area is linked by two long side corridors.

The building was completed by the end of 1874, the year the Impressionist painters held their first exhibition. This coincidence is

significant in that it reflects something of the great divide in taste and cultural attitudes at the time. The elaborate Neobaroque style used by Garnier for the Opéra reflected the taste of the nouveaux riches for work with literary and historical associations. Impressionism (at its height between about 1867 and 1886), on the other hand, abandoned Classicism for an art which seemed to be available to all, since appreciation of it required sensitivity rather than knowledge. Such anti-intellectualism pointed to a future for the common people, while Garnier's Opéra was the last flashing firework of dry academicism.

An exceedingly bright spark it was, none the less, and it remains the most attractive, inventive, and sumptuous monument to the lost luxury and grandiose cultural pretensions of nineteenth-century Paris.

THE CASTLE OF NEUSCHWANSTEIN, BAVARIA

"I propose to rebuild the ancient castle ruins near the Pöllat Falls in the genuine style of the old German knights' castles."

IN THE FOOTHILLS OF THE BAVARIAN ALPS, 50 miles (80 km) southwest of Munich, is the small, white, fairytale castle of Neuschwanstein, perched precariously on a mountain ridge with the wooded peaks behind. Framed like an ivory ornament by the dark trees, and with a nearby waterfall cascading more than 200 feet (60 m) to provide a romantic sound accompaniment, it appears like a survivor from the great medieval age of chivalry, when Teutonic knights clad in glittering armor and bearing decorated shields roamed the countryside on richly caparisoned horses.

It was such tales that inspired its builder, not in medieval times, but little more than 100 years ago. For, as King Ludwig II of Bavaria's words quoted above make clear, he had the castle built to feed his passion for such legends, particularly as interpreted in the operas of Richard Wagner.

Like that of his heroes, Ludwig's own life was both romantic and tragic. His father, Maximilian II, died in 1864, when Ludwig was 18 years old. An Austrian woman novelist described this gilded youth just after he came to the throne as "the best-looking boy I have ever seen. His tall slim figure was perfectly proportioned. With his abundant and rather curly hair…he resembled those splendid antique sculptures which first made us aware of what virile Greek manhood was like." Her opinion is confirmed by the official portraits, although they also, correctly, suggest a somewhat effeminate nature. Other reports claim that he was shy, naive, vain, generous, serious, devout, lacking in humor, but with sound judgment of character and a good memory.

THE UNDERLYING INSPIRATION for Neuschwanstein, which was built on the site of the ancient castle of Vorderhohenschwangau, were the tales of German chivalry, while its architecture was determinedly Medieval in character. The exterior of the castle – the lighted windows indicate the Singers' Hall – is mainly early Romanesque in style, and the interiors are based largely on Romanesque and Byzantine design, although the king's bedroom was ornately Gothic.

The first plans were drawn up by the court architect, Eduard Riedel, but the appearance of the castle owes most to the theater designer Christian Jank and to Ludwig himself, who closely monitored every aspect of the building and every detail of its decoration and furniture.

THE SINGERS' HALL, *the initial reason for the castle's existence, occupies the whole of one end of the top floor. On the north side is an arcaded gallery and passage, which is linked to the hall by double-columned arches (above). These are decorated with Byzantine and Celtic motifs so that, as in the rest of the castle, scarcely any surface is left without historically based decoration.*

Four huge chandeliers, suspended along the center *of the hall, and candelabra (above) along the sides, gave considerable light and heat from their 600 candles.*

IN A CASTLE where little expense was spared, Ludwig lavished the most extraordinary care and expense on the Singers' Hall. The pitched wooden ceiling has panels with ornamental designs and signs of the zodiac painted in the center, and the wooden corbels, ribs, and columns are covered in Gothic decoration and rest on carved symbolic figures. At the west end, steps lead up to three singers' bowers.

The murals in the Singers' Hall and gallery depict the saga of Parsifal and the Holy Grail, of Parsifal's son Lohengrin, and of King Arthur and the Knights of the Round Table. Scenes from other tales told in Wagner's operas decorate the walls of rooms elsewhere in the castle (*below*) – *Lohengrin* in the living room and *The Mastersingers* in the king's dressing room.

August von Heckel's mural Lohengrin's arrival at Aversa

Richard Wagner

Edward Ille's mural The mastersinger Hans Sachs with his friends

From the beginning of his reign, Ludwig was uninterested in the responsibilities of kingship and lived largely to indulge his overwhelming passion for building and for the music of Wagner and the myths and legends used in his operas. Part, at least, of this devotion is somewhat surprising, for his early music teacher said that Ludwig had no ear and could not tell a Strauss waltz from a Beethoven sonata; and even Wagner, who was nothing if not sycophantic toward the young king, said that he was completely unmusical. Nevertheless, there might have been some advantage in this to the composer, since Ludwig was not interested in the academic arguments that raged over Wagner's work and continued to admire and support him throughout his life. But the changes and tensions in their long relationship are unimportant here. What is of interest is the deep effect Wagner had on the young king.

Wagner's music even moved Ludwig physically to the extent that, at one performance of *Tannhäuser,* a courtier in the royal box noted its "almost demoniacal effect"; and when Tannhäuser re-entered the Venusberg, he observed that the king's body was so convulsed he feared an epileptic fit.

Ludwig's devotion to Wagner's music began when, only 13, he was given a copy of Wagner's *Opera and Drama* for Christmas in 1858; then, at the age of 16, he was captivated by a performance of *Lohengrin.* When he became king, with considerable financial resources, he sought out his hero Wagner at once, met him and decided to support him.

For Wagner, this could hardly have come at a better time. He was considerably in debt (an almost permanent condition with him), deeply depressed, and anxious at his failure to achieve the recognition he craved. Furthermore, when his works were staged, they were presented so inadequately that they usually failed. It was a heaven-sent situation for a wealthy patron, and Ludwig determined to be just that.

Most commentators have recorded Wagner's difficult personality, his need for a luxurious lifestyle, his dissatisfaction with his treatment by the critics, and his genuine – and frequently justifiable – dismay at productions of his work. Ludwig sought to redress Wagner's complaints throughout his life, gave

KING LUDWIG II *in the uniform of a Bavarian general. This portrait of the king, in a classic pose for great heroic figures, was painted by Ferdinand Piloty in 1865, when youthful good looks made the king an attractive subject. Piloty also painted murals at Neuschwanstein, notably in the dining room, the dressing room, and the Singers' Hall.*

IN 1886, *the year of Ludwig's death, the castle was still unfinished as this engraving shows. It also reveals the difficulties posed by the precipitous site; the wooden scaffolding must have been dangerous both to erect and to work on. Scaffolding covers the gatehouse, much of the Knights' House, and, on the other side of the courtyard, the Kemenate. And work was obviously still being carried out on the exterior of the Throne Hall, at the far left, overlooking the Alpsee and the Schwansee.*

FIFTH FLOOR

17
18

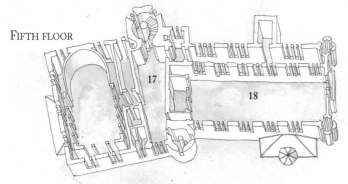

FOURTH FLOOR

7
9
16
15
14
10
11
13
8
12

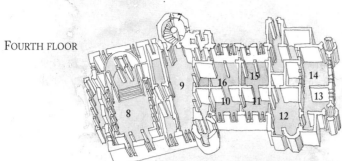

A GROUND PLAN (*bottom*) shows, from right to left, the gatehouse with its two corner towers. A gallery leads directly from the gatehouse, past the Knights' House and up steps to the castle entrance at the end of the two courtyards. The Kemenate is on the other side of the upper courtyard.

The main room on the entrance level is the kitchen, with three Romanesque columns supporting a vaulted ceiling. The vestibule, which leads to the northern staircase tower, fills the space formed by the angle of the rocky site.

Higher up (on the fourth floor), overlooking Pöllat Gorge, are the king's lavishly decorated quarters, including his bedroom, dressing room, study, and dining room. The Throne Hall, on the other side of the vestibule, rises through two stories.

Only the Singers' Hall, a vestibule, and the gallery level of the Throne Hall are found on the fifth floor. The view from the fifth-floor balcony of the Throne Hall to the mountains, more than 6,000 feet (1,800 m) in height, is the most splendid from the castle.

COMPLETE GROUND PLAN

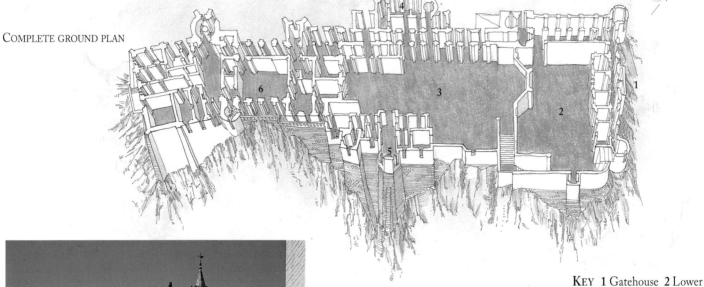

4
6
3
1
2
5

KEY 1 Gatehouse 2 Lower courtyard 3 Upper courtyard 4 Knights' House 5 Kemenate 6 Kitchen 7 Staircase tower 8 Throne Hall 9 Vestibule 10 Anteroom 11 Dining room 12 Bedroom 13 Dressing room 14 Living room 15 Study 16 Anteroom 17 Upper vestibule 18 Singers' Hall

A FLIGHT OF STEPS, *just visible on the left, leads from the lower courtyard to the upper courtyard and the entrance to the castle. The Kemenate (Ladies' Bower House) is on the left, and the Knights' House, with the long access gallery, on the right. There is a simple, almost austere, quality to the heavy Romanesque-style round-arched stonework and thick columns used for the exterior of these buildings, which are made of brick faced with square limestone slabs. The balcony on the facade is that of the Singers' Hall.*

him houses to live in, paid most of his debts, and supported his extravagances.

In return, Wagner gave Ludwig a powerful reason for living and a source for the creation of his own fantasies. In translating the old sagas of heroes and romantic deeds into a form that deeply affected and inspired the king, Wagner gave Ludwig a mission – to build what amounted to a shrine both to Wagner and to the old Teutonic knights.

Neuschwanstein, the charming toy castle built by Ludwig on the mountain ridge near Hohenschwangau, was only one of the many results of that influence. He intended the castle as an emotional tribute, primarily to the myth of Lohengrin and the Swan – Neuschwanstein means "new swan stone," and the swan symbol is found throughout the castle's decoration. It was also a practical tribute to Wagner, whose operas the king planned to stage in the Singers' Hall. This was designed as a near-replica of the Singers' Hall at Wartburg Castle, which Ludwig had visited in his youth and where, significantly, the dramatic singers' contest of 1207 takes place in *Tannhäuser*.

The castle was one of the early projects of Ludwig's reign. A manic builder, he had also begun to plan other castles and palaces inspired by Versailles after a visit to France in 1867. One, Linderhof, was nearby; another was in eastern Bavaria at Herrenchiemsee. Building proceeded on all three projects, but only Linderhof was completed before the king died. Work on Neuschwanstein, which began in 1869, continued after his death, but even today parts of the castle have not been completed: the third floor is closed to the public because it is still only bare brick. Ludwig had, however, hoped to be living at the castle three years after it was started, and in a letter to Wagner in 1868, when he was planning the project, he wrote that there would be a number of guest rooms, adding: "You will know who the guest is whom I want to invite and entertain there."

It is, perhaps, not surprising that the castle was not finished. Its building was a considerable problem even for the energetic, inventive and enthusiastic nineteenth-century architects and engineers who had created some of the greatest buildings in Europe, and the early skyscrapers in North America. The first

THE KING'S BEDROOM, *decorated in elaborate late-Gothic style, is quite different from the other rooms in the castle; the bed, surmounted by an arched canopy, looks like a memorial tomb in a medieval church. The murals show scenes from the story of Tristan and Isolde, statues of whom also appear at the corners of the tiled stove. The symbol of the swan appears in fabrics and tapestries, and the silver wash bowl is filled from a silver swan fountain.*

SCENES FROM THE LEGEND *of Tannhäuser, including "Tannhäuser's arrival at the Wartburg" and a voluptuous painting of "Tannhäuser at the Court of Venus," adorn the walls of the small study. Only the finest materials were used throughout the castle: the hangings were embroidered silk; the furniture and paneling in both bedroom and study were made from knot-free oak.*

THE THRONE HALL, *which rises through two stories and is arcaded on both, is the most impressive in the palace after the Singers' Hall. The sumptuous decoration is mainly Byzantine in style, with some echoes of the great Sancta Sophia in Istanbul. Suspended from the center of the ceiling – a flattened blue dome spangled with stars – is a great chandelier in the form of a Byzantine crown.*

By contrast, the patterning of the wall surfaces is reminiscent of both Romanesque and Celtic designs, and the tessellated floor is inlaid with ornamental patterns, plants, and animals. The murals all have Christian associations and include "Christ in his Glory with St. John, Mary and Angels," "The Twelve Apostles," and "St. George."

THE STAIRCASE TOWER *in the angle of the building on the north side gives access to all levels. Over the top landing, a starry cupola, which echoes the ceiling in the Throne Hall, floats above a marble column in the form of a palm tree. This gives a bizarre, lighthearted touch to the Byzantine decoration of the octagonal stairhead.*

difficulty at Neuschwanstein was the site's inaccessibility, the second its nature – a rugged peak on which there was an old watch tower – chosen by Ludwig because of its closeness to the Schwansee. The tower, as well as 20 feet (6 m) of solid rock, had first to be blasted off the top of the ridge to provide a platform on which the castle could stand. This was intended to rise out of the rock as if part of it, which made even the erection of the wooden scaffolding an immense problem.

A third difficulty was Ludwig's constantly changing requirements for the interior. If the exterior presents a Medieval dream in three dimensions, the interior is a fantasy of architectural styles and a riot of pictorial mythology and elaborate furnishings. The king demanded a standard of work and a schedule that it was almost impossible to meet; so it is, in many ways, astounding that the building advanced as quickly and as far as it did.

The castle is approached by a winding road among trees, which conceal it until one rounds the final bend and is confronted by the red sandstone gatehouse with its Gothic entrance. Little of the castle is visible at this point, and it is only as the visitor passes from the lower courtyard into the upper that the facade of the castle comes into view. The building rises to six stories. Of these the second floor and the king's quarters on the top two floors were more or less completed when he died.

Ludwig's death was a sad end to a life that had begun with such glittering promise. In mid-1886 he was declared mentally deranged and unable to carry out his governmental duties. There was a history of mental instability in the Wittelsbach family, but Ludwig's devotion to his romantic dreams, along with the pressures imposed by his various ministers, his lack of interest in affairs of state, and his dislike of court life must have contributed to his sense of isolation and increasing eccentricity, which was interpreted as evidence of a

MEDIEVAL CASTLES were generally built on easily defensible sites to provide a refuge for their owners. Neuschwanstein effectively fulfilled this demand for Ludwig. The isolation of his medieval fantasy could hardly be more tellingly revealed than it is in this view of the castle, rising dreamlike through the morning mist, a "fabric of enchantment piled to Heaven."

deteriorating mental condition. Later photographs show a physical deterioration as well.

On June 12, 1886, by order of the newly appointed regent, his uncle Prince Luitpold, Ludwig was taken from Neuschwanstein to Berg Castle on Lake Starnberg, some 20 miles (32 km) from Munich. It was at Berg that Ludwig had lived during his early enthusiasm for Wagner and had rented a villa for the composer, so the place had especially happy memories for him. At about 6 p.m. on the day after his arrival, Ludwig and his doctor went for a walk. Shortly after 10 p.m., following a hectic search, their bodies were found in shallow water close to the shore of the lake. The king's watch had stopped at 6:54. Was it suicide, murder, or accident? No one knows.

These notes are arranged chronologically in a sequence related to the chapters in the book. Monticello is not included since only Jefferson was closely concerned with it, and details of his life are covered in the main text.

St. Peter's, Rome
The Popes of the Renaissance

The papacy is the only institution that has existed continuously since the time of the Roman Empire, when Peter, the first father of the Church (pope=*papa*=father), established the pope as the head of the living Church of Christ. There have been many saintly popes, some nonentities, not a few worthless or bad, but the papacy has always been greater than its incumbent. During the Renaissance period, these varying characteristics were all evident – with, perhaps, a greater percentage of the bad than at other times.

The nature of the Renaissance ethos was such as to inspire a worldly self-absorption from which popes were not immune. Human achievement and fame were replacing the official spiritual otherworldliness of the medieval period. The individualism of the artist was recognized and celebrated, while ambitious rulers paraded their personal wealth and power. It is hardly surprising, therefore, that Renaissance popes had personal ambitions for the secular power of the Church, as well as being involved in the intellectual pursuits of the day. Although their real power lay in the authority of the Church and the papacy, they behaved as Renaissance princes. The result was that the most effective popes were worldly, ambitious, intellectual, learned, and, usually, fiercely defensive of the authority of the papacy.

Pope Nicholas V (1397–1455)

The first essentially "humanist" pope, Nicholas V was driven by a desire to rebuild the decaying city of Rome and by an intellectual determination to reestablish the qualities of Classical societies. He virtually founded the great Vatican library and began work on the Cathedral Church of St. Peter, employing Bernardo Rossellino to prepare plans, which were never executed. But his was the initial inspiration. Following him, Sixtus IV, pope from 1471 to 1484, fostered humanism, built the Sistine Chapel, and continued work on St. Peter's.

Pope Julius II (1443–1513)

The papacy is usually a short-term office that often comes late in life, and by the time a pope is enthroned he is of mature mind with fixed notions and, probably, diminished energy. When Julius II, the nephew of Sixtus IV, was elevated to the papacy in 1503, he was 60 years old and lived only another 10 years, but his influence on the rebuilding of St. Peter's was seminal, because he brought his enormous creative energy and strength of purpose to bear on the project.

Julius provides a singular example of a Renaissance pope, for he was largely concerned with the reestablishment of papal sovereignty over the Church's old territories. He was at the same time a liberal patron of the arts, notably by employing Michelangelo to decorate the ceiling of the Sistine Chapel and to provide the design for Julius's tomb. In addition, Raphael was called upon to paint the Stanze in Julius's private apartments and Bramante to provide a complete new design for St. Peter's. Since much of Bramante's design was incorporated into the finished structure, Julius's impact during his short tenure was memorable.

Pope Paul III (1468–1549)

When Paul III was made pope in 1534, 20 years had passed during which little progress had been made. Already 68 years old, Paul nevertheless carried on the work begun by Julius, appointing Michelangelo as architect of St. Peter's. By temperament and desire a Renaissance prince, he advanced his young nephews to cardinals and tried to aggrandize his illegitimate sons. The evident need for Church reform inhibited this, and during his time the Inquisition was reconstituted in Italy, censorship was established, and the Society of Jesus (the Jesuits) gained acceptance. In 1542, Paul convened a general council (known as the Council of Trent) which met in 1545 at Trento in northern Italy and was responsible for starting the Counter-Reformation. When Paul died in 1549, Michelangelo had advanced the work on St. Peter's to the stage where it was evident that it would, in time, be completed.

Pope Paul V (1552–1621)

The later stages of the Renaissance papacy were much concerned with the consolidation of the reforms introduced at the Council of Trent, but by the beginning of the 17th century, during the pontificate of Paul V, further work on St. Peter's (the extension of the nave and the addition of the facade by Carlo Maderno) was accompanied by the pope's active participation in promoting Catholicism internationally. He was succeeded by Urban VIII, who appointed Bernini as architect of St. Peter's, initiating the final stages of the new Cathedral Church of St. Peter.

Pope Alexander VII (1610–91)

The last pope with whom the rebuilding of St. Peter's was linked was Alexander VII, a man of fine, but indolent, character, who left most of the administration of the Church to the congregation, which resulted in a reduction of the palpable power of the papacy. Alexander's pontificate coincided with the completion of the work on the church and marked the start of a less nepotistic period as the influence of the administration increased.

Donato Bramante (*c.*1444–1514)

Much is obscure about Bramante's origins, including the year of his birth. The nickname Bramante, the Italian for "ardent" or "intensely desiring," had been attached to his grandfather and appears to have descended to him.

Despite this mysterious background, he was to become the embodiment of the most austere expression of the Renaissance in Roman architecture. His most famous building, the so-called Tempietto in Rome, is regarded as the model for detail and proportion on which his contemporaries based much of their design standards. His designs for St. Peter's are the subject of considerable academic inquiry, but it appears certain that he set the pattern for the great domed building eventually achieved by Michelangelo. He was buried in the old Church of St. Peter, but his grave was destroyed during work on the rebuilding.

Michelangelo Buonarroti (1475–1564)

One of the most important figures in the history of Western art, Michelangelo was a painter, sculptor, and architect, and his achievements in all these fields represented the zenith of the High Renaissance, introduced the elements of Mannerism, and presaged the Baroque. He was recognized as the most powerful and dominant creative force in his own time; and his energy, single-mindedness, irascibility, and suspicious nature marked him as a figure apart.

Michelangelo was born in Caprese in Tuscany and grew up in Florence, the city in which much of his early work was done. The painter Domenico Ghirlandaio, his first master, introduced him to the great Renaissance merchant prince and patron, Lorenzo de' Medici (the Magnificent), through whom he was launched on his career.

He always described himself as a sculptor, and it was in this art form that his creative energy was at its most evident. Nevertheless, his architectural achievement, which culminated in his work on St. Peter's, was a singular and significant contribution to the spirit of the High Renaissance. His architectural career began with the Medici Chapel in Florence when he was 45 years of age, but most of his architecture was produced during his later period in Rome; until his last years, it remained an activity peripheral to the many sculptural commissions he received.

In 1503, Pope Julius II summoned him to Rome, and after 1534, he spent much time there on great architectural projects such as the Capitol (Piazza del Campidoglio); the Palazzo Farnese, the greatest city palace of the time; the Porta Pia (the new city gate); and the designs for the new St. Peter's. Michelangelo was deeply religious, and his architecture expressed the sense of awe, grandeur, and splendor that characterized the Church of his time in a way no other artist achieved; it seemed also to express his own prodigious natural abilities.

Carlo Maderno (1556–1629)

In the period between the end of the High Renaissance and the introduction of 17th-century Roman Baroque, Maderno was the most outstanding architect working in Rome. Although he designed a number of important religious and secular buildings, he is best remembered for extending the nave and providing the screen facade on St. Peter's. His role as a link between the two periods is

appropriately symbolized by his imposing facade, which separates the main body of the church and the dome by Michelangelo from the great Baroque piazza by Bernini.

Much of his early work was of a practical nature – engineering works such as bridges and aqueducts – but as a result of remodeling the facade of the medieval church of St. Susanna in Rome between 1593 and 1603, he became established as one of the first Baroque architects.

Gianlorenzo Bernini (1598–1680)

Like Michelangelo, Bernini, the last of the great universal artists of the Italian Renaissance, was a painter, sculptor, and architect, but of a very different temperament. A man of charm, sophistication, and wit, he characterized this period, the Roman Baroque, as his great predecessor had the High Renaissance. His astonishing abilities were recognized early, and by his late teens, he was already famous as a sculptor. His facility and sensibility as a carver in marble have never been surpassed, and he rivals Michelangelo in historical reputation.

Bernini's first patron was Cardinal Scipione Borghese, whose commissions for sculptures established the artist's reputation and brought him to the attention of Cardinal Maffeo Barberini, who became his close friend. When Barberini became Pope Urban VIII in 1623, he aspired to secure Bernini's fame as a second Michelangelo – dominant in all the arts. For Urban, Bernini designed the *baldacchino* in St. Peter's, as well as other architectural works. After Urban's death, he was employed by private patrons until the accession of Pope Alexander VII (Fabio Chigi), who consistently employed him and for whom he designed the great piazza. Indeed, one of Bernini's last works was the tomb of his patron in St. Peter's.

By this time, Bernini's fame was such that he was commanded by King Louis XIV of France to come to Paris to rebuild the Louvre Palace; the project was not completed, and the sole result of the visit was the famous marble bust of the king.

It is difficult to overestimate the importance of Bernini's career. As a sculptor, he was the supreme portraitist, and his subtle carved rendering in marble of the fleshy surface of the human body remains unequaled. In his architecture, he mastered traditional Renaissance design and – in a personal combination of sculptural and architectural elements – added to it an emotional content expressive of the high sentiment of the Counter-Reformation.

Buckingham Palace, London
King George III (1738–1820)

The first Hanoverian ruler to speak English fluently, George III succeeded his grandfather George II as king of Great Britain. He was devoted to Britain and had a genuine, deep love of his people. He was in turn revered and

respected by them, his keen interest in agriculture earning him the nickname Farmer George. He bought Buckingham House for his young queen, Charlotte, and, as The Queen's House, it became their family home.

From 1765, George suffered from the disease porphyria, which caused periodic and increasingly serious bouts of madness, and by 1811 he had lapsed into permanent insanity. His son, the Prince of Wales, then became Prince Regent, inaugurating what is known as the Regency style in art and architecture, and when the king died both mad and blind in 1820, the Prince Regent succeeded him.

George III is, perhaps, best known for the failure of his political aims and in particular for his policy regarding the American colonies. This was so disastrous that in 1776 they declared their independence, which was ratified in 1783.

King George IV (1762–1830)

The eldest son of George III, who became Prince Regent in 1811, ascended the throne in 1820 on the king's death. His character was hardly admirable, and he continued as king much as he had done as Prince Regent, leading a profligate, irresponsible, and arrogant life which made him a figure of public scorn. His relationship with his wife Caroline was stormy from the outset, and they parted within one year of their marriage in 1795.

Not only was he a dissolute king, but he also inspired disgust with the Georgian type of monarchy. His employment of John Nash in great architectural work in the center of London and on The Queen's House, which George renamed Buckingham Palace, was almost his only significant achievement.

Queen Victoria (1819–1901)

Victoria, the granddaughter of George III, succeeded to the throne at the age of 18 in 1837, on the death of her uncle William IV. In 1840 she married her cousin Albert, the son of the Duke of Saxe-Coburg Gotha, who was her own age. Almost from the beginning of her reign, she showed remarkable firmness of purpose. Before their marriage, Albert wrote that she was said to be "incredibly stubborn" and that "she delights in court ceremonies, etiquette and trivial formalities."

Victoria's initial popularity, largely due to her youth, was damaged by some ill-advised early actions, and it was considered essential that she should marry someone who could give her safe advice. The serious young Prince Albert soon justified his role and quickly became the queen's only adviser, effectively her private secretary, and the love of her life. After his death in 1861, she retreated into a reclusive life, devoting herself to the role of constitutional monarch as envisaged by Prince Albert, and revealing in the process how well she had learned the business of state from him.

During her reign, the British Empire reached

the apogee of its power and influence, and by the time of her death, she had established her reign not only as the longest in British history, but also as a period that was to carry her name worldwide and seemed to express her character. As one writer on Victorian England has expressed it, the British monarchy had acquired "in place of a definite but brittle prerogative, an indefinable but potent influence." Through her character as much as her long life, she restored the dignity and popularity of the monarchy, and in making it respectable seemed to assure the continuance of the institution.

By establishing Buckingham Palace as her residence in London from the beginning of her reign, she also made sure that it became one of the best-loved and most revered royal palaces in the modern world.

John Nash (1752–1835)

The principal architect concerned in converting Buckingham House into Buckingham Palace, John Nash was born in London, although he was of Welsh descent. After a period in the office of an important London architect, he married and set up on his own as a speculative builder. After early failures, his ambitious nature and prodigious energy enabled him to become a fashionable architect and builder.

His designs for Regent's Park, Regent Street, and a number of houses in central London made him a natural choice for the redesign of Buckingham House, particularly since in 1813 he had become the Prince Regent's private architect. For the prince he also designed the Royal Pavilion in Brighton (in "Indian style"), remodeled Carlton House, the residence of the present Queen Mother, and replanned and replanted St. James's Park, which fronts Buckingham Palace. From 1829 he was a sick man, having probably suffered a stroke, and in 1834 he retired to the Isle of Wight where, in East Cowes, he died a year later.

Nash was a man of great creative drive, not deeply concerned with subtle refinements or the highest qualities of craftsmanship, but his impact on the character of central London is still evident, and he is remembered as one of England's greatest architects.

OPÉRA GARNIER, PARIS
Emperor Napoleon III (1808–73)

Louis Napoleon, as he was originally known, was born in Paris the son of Louis Bonaparte, the brother of Emperor Napoleon I. He was an ardent liberal in the Bonapartist cause and came to regard himself as the leading representative of his family and the putative emperor of France – a highly unlikely eventuality, since France was a republic.

A bold, adventurous optimist, he conspired toward that end from his base in London (where he lived when Queen Victoria acceded to the throne in 1837), but his early activities were unsuccessful. Imprisoned in France, he escaped in 1846 back to London where he again engaged in complicated, but on this occasion successful, political and military intrigue until, in December 1848, as Louis Napoleon, he was elected President of the Second Republic. In his mind, this was only a stepping stone to imperial power. And through a carefully prepared and executed coup d'état, he finally succeeded, in December 1852, in becoming Emperor Napoleon III.

During the next decade, much of his time and energy was devoted to the remodeling of Paris, which included the construction of the new opera house designed by Garnier. But his opportunistic foreign policy and style of leadership resulted, in July 1870, in his declaring war on Prussia. This disastrous enterprise ended in defeat for France and the occupation of Paris by the Germans. Before this, in September 1870, the Second Empire had collapsed, and Napoleon had joined his exiled wife Eugénie in the small town of Chislehurst in southern England, where he died two years later.

Georges-Eugène Haussmann (1809–91)

Born in Paris of a bourgeois Protestant Bonapartist family (his grandfather was a Napoleonic general), Haussmann was essentially a Parisian, educated at the Lycée, the Bourbon College, and the Law School of the University of Paris. His great energy, creative imagination, powerful temperament, and Bonapartist loyalty made him an ideal collaborator when Louis Napoleon became President of the Second Republic. After appointments as Préfect (governor) in politically sensitive areas of France, he was recalled to Paris in 1853 by Louis Napoleon (now Emperor Napoleon III) to direct his replanning of the city.

During the next 17 years, Haussmann carried out the most extensive reconstruction of a city in modern history. Napoleon's three main objectives were to make Paris a magnificent imperial capital; to redesign the city for population growth and industrialization; and, significantly, to make Paris a secure seat of government capable of suppressing insurrection. Haussmann ruthlessly carried through this unprecedented and extreme assignment until his dismissal in 1870. His greatest attainment in transforming Paris into a modern city was that he succeeded in melding the new with the old so that Paris is a living city with centuries of history but with a modern aura.

Charles Garnier (1825–98)

Jean-Louis-Charles Garnier's fame depends upon one building, the Paris Opéra. It demanded all his considerable energy and ingenuity for the 15 years between his winning the competition for the design in 1861 to the completion of the building's lavish interior in 1875. Although he was responsible for a number of other buildings, most notably the Casino at Monte Carlo, the Opéra remains his monument and the most significant example of mid-19th century French Neobaroque.

Born in Paris, he was apprenticed to an architectural draftsman and later went to a drawing school where he met Jean-Baptiste Carpeaux, who became a lifelong friend and collaborator and the most famous and talented contributor to the decoration of the Opéra.

In 1848 Garnier won the prestigious Grand Prix de Rome and spent the next five years in that city. There he met other students who also became collaborators on the Opéra, notably Paul Baudry, responsible for the ceiling paintings in the foyer, and Jules-Eugène Lenepveu, who painted the original ceiling in the auditorium.

Garnier's design for the Opéra was so much loved by the Parisian public when it was completed that he became a greatly respected and famous figure. His career was, however, at an architecturally creative end, and, during the remaining 23 years of his life, he built nothing of comparable distinction. His first great work was, thus, also his last, but it was on such a spectacular scale and of such imaginative grandeur that it excited the whole international architectural profession for a generation and is still a magnet for visitors to Paris.

Jean-Baptise Carpeaux (1827–75)

Before moving to Paris where he studied sculpture with a notable and popular sculptor, François Rude, Carpeaux studied architecture at Valenciennes, his birthplace. Rude's most famous sculpture is *The Marseilles, or the Departure of the Volunteers* on the Arc de Triomphe in Paris, a work of realism, movement, and vitality whose influence is evident in Carpeaux's sculpture. To this vitality, Carpeaux added a sensitive delicacy seen in his most famous work, *The Dance*, on the facade of the Paris Opéra. He was also noted for his portrait busts, which show a fine perception of skin and clothing and great animation of expression.

NEUSCHWANSTEIN, BAVARIA
The Wittelsbach Dynasty

King Ludwig II, the creator of the castle of Neuschwanstein, was one of the last members of the ancient Wittelsbach family to rule the Bavarian state in southern Germany that contains the cities of Munich, Nuremberg, Würzburg, and Regensburg.

The family took its name from the castle of Wittelsbach, near Archach in Bavaria, when Count Otto V moved to the castle in 1124. The connection was consolidated at the end of the 12th century, when Otto VI became Duke of Bavaria, and lasted until the revolution of 1918 overthrew the Wittelsbach dynasty and replaced it with a republic. The coup was organized by Kurt Eisner, a radical journalist who had contrived to make himself president.

Architectural Styles

For those not familiar with architectural terms, the following information will be helpful in understanding some of the styles referred to in this book.

Classical Architecture

This includes the architecture of the civilizations of ancient Greece and Rome. Greek civilization, which dates back to 1000 B.C., covered mainland Greece and the islands of the Aegean, and included some settlements in Asia Minor and Italy. Its architecture reached its highest point during the 5th century B.C., at which time the Parthenon was built.

Roman civilization began, traditionally, with the foundation of Rome in 753 B.C. and expanded during succeeding centuries to become, by the time of its decline in the 5th century A.D., the greatest power in the then known world. Through its colonization of Europe, it spread the Classical spirit to the extent that this has remained the dominant architectural inspiration of Western culture.

The Classical Orders

Classical architecture is identified by the five orders, or styles, three of which are Greek and two Roman. They are similar in use, but are distinguished by decorative differences and by the relative proportions of the elements.

The orders are identified by reference to the column and the entablature. The column has three parts: the base, the shaft, and the capital. The entablature is the part above the column and consists of the architrave (the horizontal beam), the frieze (the middle section, often decorated with relief sculpture), and the cornice (the upper section). The capital (the feature between the shaft of the column and the entablature) consists of the echinus (the sloped or curved molding) and the abacus (the square slab above the echinus). In all the Greek orders, the column is fluted, that is, it has curved vertical channeling. The illustrations below show only the tops of the columns and the entablatures – the most easily identified elements – the bases, with one exception, are largely similar.

The Greek orders are always placed in their supposed sequence of development as follows:

Doric

The first of the orders, with an undecorated capital. It was distinguished from all other orders by the fact that the fluted column had no molded base, but stood directly on the stylobate, or stepped platform. The later, Roman, Doric was also usually fluted but had a base.

Ionic

The proportions of this order were less sturdy than those of the Doric; for example, the column was more slender relative to its height. There was also a molded base pad. The Doric and Ionic were initially used separately, but in later buildings, they were often combined. For instance, Doric columns can be found supporting Ionic sculpted friezes, or Ionic columns used within an otherwise Doric building.

Corinthian

The most elaborate order of Greek architecture was less frequently used than either Doric or Ionic, partly because it was regarded by the Greeks as too undignified to be used in colonnades.

The Romans took over the Greek orders, adapting them to their different, less austere, view. They also employed two more.

Tuscan

The simplest of all the orders, the Tuscan is believed to have developed from Etruscan temples. It had a molded base, a plain column without fluting, and an undecorated capital.

Composite

As its name implies, the Composite order is a combination of Ionic volutes and Corinthian decorative plant forms. Like most Roman architecture, it is more decoratively elaborate than the Greek form from which it is adapted.

Trabeation and Arcuation

All early Western civilizations, from the time of the Egyptians to the present day, have adopted one or both of the basic forms of building construction known as trabeation and arcuation.

Trabeation employs beams, or lintels, supported by posts (columns) or walls to create the structure. It is the method most widely used in Greek architecture, for example in the Parthenon (*see illustration page 6*), and is also common in all subsequent architecture. A stable and strong method of construction, it depends only on the strength of the materials used. When stone is the material for both posts and beams, the posts must be close together, since stone is subject to fracture over longer distances. A combination of wooden beams and stone supports covers larger areas more effectively.

Where bigger open areas were required, the solution was found in the building form known as arcuation: the use of the arch and its expression in circular form as a dome, or in continuous form as a barrel vault. The arch, dome, and vault were widely used by the Romans, who also continued to employ trabeation, often in conjunction with domed structures, as in the Pantheon in Rome (*see illustration page 7*).

The Greeks appear to have regarded the arch as unsuitable for public buildings, but they used

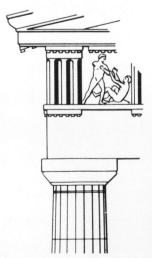

Doric

Here the architrave is a simple slab beam, while the frieze along the middle of the entablature contains triglyphs (vertically channeled blocks) and metopes (sculpted or plain blocks) alternately. The cornice includes the sloping part of the pediment formed by the triangular end of a building with a pitched roof.

Ionic

The elements here are clearly divided, and the frieze contains a continuous sculpture. The identifying feature is the capital composed of two spiral forms, or volutes, with a decorative element, the echinus, linking them at the lower part.

it in engineering works, such as drains, and in other non-visible structures. The Romans were ingenious engineers and were able to overcome some of the inherent structural difficulties of arch construction. While the beam is a stable single element applying only downward pressure on its support, the arch is composed of a number of elements in the form of tapered stones, which apply a downward and outward thrust that has to be contained.

A variety of methods may be employed to accomplish this, such as a continuous chain around the base of the drum/dome as is found in St. Paul's Cathedral, London (*see illustration page 9*). The most usual method, however, is to buttress the walls so that they can withstand the outward thrust or, in the case of bridges, to set the walls in solid ground at each end.

Medieval Architecture

Early in the fourth century A.D., the Roman Empire under Constantine officially adopted Christianity. This enabled the rapid expansion of the religion throughout all Rome's dominions and opened the way for the building of churches to replace Roman temples. Christian forms of worship demanded new stylistic characteristics in architecture. In the next 1,000 years, it developed into what is known as the Medieval style – the architecture of the Middle Ages.

During its development, several sub-styles appeared. The most important of these were Gothic and Romanesque, but others included Early English, Flamboyant, and Perpendicular. In simple terms, earlier styles used the Roman arch and barrel vault, while later developments resulted in high, pointed arches, complicated vaulting patterns, and soaring spires, crockets, and finials, as seen in Salisbury Cathedral (*see illustration page 8*). This was also the time of great castle building on defensible raised ground. By the 19th century, this period evoked much nostalgia and resulted in a return to medievalism and such extravaganzas as Neuschwanstein.

Renaissance Architecture

The word Renaissance means "rebirth" and in this context denotes the revival of the Classical forms of art and architecture used in the Greek and Roman civilizations. This new interest followed the Medieval period of Christian-inspired art.

Renaissance art forms appeared first in Italy and quickly spread to the rest of Europe. Although Renaissance style is usually divided into several categories, the underlying Classical influence has remained the most potent and dominant force in determining the character of all subsequent art and architecture up to the present. Four of the five buildings discussed in this book are Classically inspired.

Baroque Architecture

European art and architecture during the 17th century and most of the 18th century is termed Baroque. In this style, the Classical forms characteristic of the Renaissance were used in a new spirit of elaboration and exaggeration to express the sophistication and structural complexity endemic to the period.

The origin of the term has been related both to a Portuguese word *barroco*, an imperfect, irregularly shaped pearl, and to the Italian *baroca*, used in medieval disputation to signify an illogicality or a flaw in an argument. From this it became, in 16th-century Italy and France, a term for convoluted processes of thought. Its use in relation to the arts began in the 18th century, when it was defined in terms of its opposition to Classicism as extravagant, willful, disregarding the rules of proportion, and with everything dependent on the whim of the artist.

One critic, in 1797, wrote that "Baroque is the ultimate in the bizarre." Today the term is used to describe both the period and the extension of the Classical language of art and architecture. The most obvious and finest examples in this book are found in the work of Bernini in St. Peter's, Rome.

Palladianism

The highly important influence of the late Renaissance architect Andrea Palladio (1508–80) is reflected in the adoption of the term "Palladian" in the early 18th century to describe a form of Classically based architecture. The architect Inigo Jones introduced Palladianism to Britain, but it was the Earl of Burlington who ensured its acceptance by designing houses for his friends and Chiswick House for himself.

Palladio's influence is evident in two of the buildings in this book. Monticello, Thomas Jefferson's house; John Nash's early 19th-century designs for Buckingham Palace; and even Sir Aston Webb's 20th-century facade on the Mall in London contain much that is Palladian.

Palladio translated the public, official architecture of Greece and Rome into an attractive, comfortable, distinguished, and distinctive domestic form. He owes much of his influence to his architectural "pattern book," *The Four Books of Architecture,* published first in Italian in 1570 and subsequently in English and French. In this work he made many drawings of Classical buildings, some of his own design, which formed the basic primer for Palladian architecture.

Neoclassicism & Neobaroque

In an architectural context, these stylistic terms represent extensions in the late 18th and the 19th centuries of Classical and Baroque forms. Neoclassicism was a careful, academically inspired return to the purer Classical temple form after the "inventions" of Palladianism and is seen in such buildings as the Altes Museum, Berlin, by Karl Friedrich Schinkel.

Neobaroque is not properly a style, but more an indication of the extravagant, emotionally charged Baroque quality found in a few mid-19th century buildings. The Opéra Garnier is the most significant example in France, and there is none in Britain that could justly be described as Neobaroque.

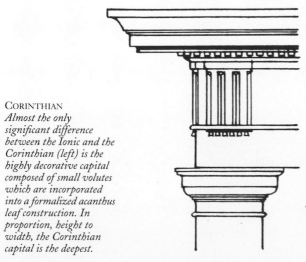

CORINTHIAN
Almost the only significant difference between the Ionic and the Corinthian (left) is the highly decorative capital composed of small volutes which are incorporated into a formalized acanthus leaf construction. In proportion, height to width, the Corinthian capital is the deepest.

TUSCAN
In this order, there is no fluting on the column and the base is molded. The elements of the echinus and the abacus are similar to those of the Doric.

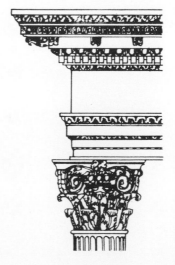

COMPOSITE
Although the Ionic volute appears as a small element in the Greek Corinthian order, it is emphatically present in the Roman Composite. Apart from the capital, the order is similar in proportion and character to the Corinthian.

INDEX

Acknowledgments

Picture credits

t = top *b* = bottom *c* = center *r* = right *l* = left

2*l* G. Gräfenhain/Britstock-IFA; 2*r* Robert Lautman; 2/3 C. Bowman/Robert Harding Picture Library; 3*l* Kotoh/Zefa Picture Library; 3*r* Hans Peter Merten/Tony Stone Images; 5*t* AKG London; 5*c* Guildhall Library; 5*b* AKG London; 6 Trewin Copplestone; 7 Eric Back/Britstock-IFA; 8*t* Trewin Copplestone; 8*b* John Miller/Robert Harding Picture Library; 9/12*t* Trewin Copplestone; 12*b* C.L. Schmidt/Britstock-IFA; 13 AKG London; 15*t* Robert Harding Picture Library; 15*b*/20*t* Scala; 20*b* Spectrum Colour Library; 22*t* Scala; 22*b* Adam Woolfitt/Robert Harding Picture Library; 22–23 Spectrum Colour Library; 23 Charles C. Place/The Image Bank; 24 G. Gräfenhain/Britstock-IFA; 27 Langdon Clay; 30*t* Robert Lautman; 30*b* Langdon Clay; 32*t* Courtesy of the Thomas Jefferson Memorial Foundation; gift of Mr. and Mrs. Carl W. Smith and Mr. and Mrs. T. Eugene Worrell; 32*b* Langdon Clay; 34*t* E.T. Archive; 34*b*/35 Langdon Clay; 36 Robert Lautman; 37 Guildhall Library; 39*t* Roy Miles Gallery/The Bridgeman Art Library; 39*b* Forbes Magazine Collection, New York/The Bridgeman Art Library; 42*t* John Freeman/The Royal Collection © Her Majesty Queen Elizabeth II; 42*b* The Royal Collection © Her Majesty Queen Elizabeth II; 44*t* Jesus College, Oxford; 44*b* Jeremy Whitaker/The Royal Collection © Her Majesty Queen Elizabeth II; 45 Camera Press; 46*t* Jeremy Whitaker/The Royal Collection © Her Majesty Queen Elizabeth II; 46*b* A.F. Kersting/The Royal Collection © Her Majesty Queen Elizabeth II; 47 John Freeman/The Royal Collection © Her Majesty Queen Elizabeth II; 48 C. Bowman/Robert Harding Picture Library; 49 AKG London; 51*t* Robert Harding Picture Library; 51*b* Jacques Moatti/Explorer/Robert Harding Picture Library; 54*t* Giraudon/The Bridgeman Art Library; 54*b* Jacques Moatti/Explorer/Robert Harding Picture Library; 56 Musée des Beaux-Arts, Valenciennes/The Bridgeman Art Library; 58/59 Jacques Moatti/Explorer/ Robert Harding Picture Library; 60 Kotoh/Zefa Picture Library; 61 AKG London; 63*t* Robert Harding Picture Library; 63*b* Alan Clifton/Camera Press; 66*t* E.T. Archive; 66*c* FPG/Robert Harding Picture Library; 66*b* E.T. Archive; 68 AKG London; 69 Robert Harding Picture Library; 70*t* Bumann/Britstock-IFA; 70*b* Hureb/Britstock-IFA; 71 Robert Harding Picture Library; 72 Hans Peter Merten/Tony Stone Images

Artwork credits
Robert Nelmes 21, 33, 45, 56–57, 69
John Hutchinson 57*b*

Editorial director Sophie Collins
Managing editor Lindsay McTeague
Copy editors Isabella Raeburn, Maggi McCormick
DTP editors Mary Pickles, Pennie Jelliff
Production editor Sorrel Everton
U.S. editor Mary Ann Lynch
Index Caroline Sheard
Production Sarah Hinks